A PALE HORSE RIDES

Shawn Boonstra

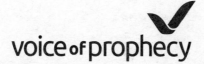

voice of prophecy

and Pacific Press Publishing Association

Cover Illustration & Design by Palmer Halvorson
Interior Design by Mark Bond
Text Typeset: Minion Pro

Copyright © 2017 by the Voice of Prophecy. All Rights Reserved.

Additional copies of *A Pale Horse Rides,* resources mentioned in this book's
footnotes, and many other spiritual resources are available by calling toll-free
1-844-822-2943 or by visiting vop.com/store.

Unless otherwise marked, all Scripture verses are quoted from NKJV,
the New King James Version®. Copyright © 1982 by Thomas Nelson, Inc.
Used by permission. All rights reserved.

Printed in the United States of America by
Pacific Press Publishing Association, Nampa, Idaho.

www.pacificpress.com

ISBN: 978-0-8163-6345-2

CONTENTS

So I looked, and behold, a pale horse.

And the name of him who sat on it was

Death, and Hades followed with him. And

power was given to them over a fourth of

the earth, to kill with sword, with hunger,

with death, and by the beasts of the earth.

(Revelation 6:8)

PREFACE

COMPOSING A HISTORICAL NARRATIVE CAN BE A tricky business. The writer must pick and choose which elements to highlight, and which ones can safely be left on the cutting room floor. What follows is a story that plays out over more than 1,000 years, and the reader can see, from the rather short nature of the book, that much has been left unsaid.

In this case, *very* much has been left unsaid. I have waded through countless thousands of pages in order to ferret out the story you are about to read, and I have had to make painful decisions about what to mention, and what to leave out. Wherever possible, I have consulted the oldest and most original sources available, at some expense. A great deal of detective work has gone into constructing the grand sweep of history you are about to read, and I believe the facts as presented to be accurate.

This is, however, not intended to be the final word on the subject by any stretch of the imagination. This book was written as a companion piece for the video series, *A Pale Horse Rides*, and scarcely touches the topic. It is meant as a very brief introduction—a means by which the reader's interest will be piqued enough to continue studying. It is very nearly a simple timeline. I highly recommend that the you peruse the bibliography at the end and avail yourself of some of the books mentioned.

Those looking for a comprehensive biography of Luther will surely be disappointed; we have only the space required to touch on the highlights of his incredible contribution to Christendom. At the top of the list for recommended reading is Roland Bainton's landmark book, *Here I Stand*, which is widely available in many editions. Also of special note are J. A. Wylie's *History of the Waldenses,* Augustus Neander's *General History of the Christian Religion and Church* (this will keep you busy for a very long time), Jean-Henri Merle d'Aubigné's *History of the Reformation*, Thomas Cahill's *How the Irish Saved Civilization,* and Leslie Hardinge's *The Celtic Church in Britain.* This is not to disparage the other titles or diminish their importance; I have read them all for a reason. I also recommend, for those wishing to place this narrative in the larger historical context, E. G. White's *The Great Controversy*, which does not appear in the bibliography but does a magnificent job of tracing the prophetic threads of history from the 1st century to the present day.

Much of this account is a story not often told, and the time seems ripe to begin telling it again.

—Shawn Boonstra
Colorado, August 2017

CHAPTER ONE:
C. 400 BC

NOBODY IS REALLY SURE WHY, ABOUT 400 YEARS before Christ, the Celts suddenly decided to cross the Alps into the Po valleys in the north of Italy. Usually, when people groups migrate, it is a matter of survival—a search for better lands with more abundant resources. Perhaps in this case, climate change was to blame. Rising temperatures in Europe caused smaller bodies of water to dry up, leaving behind mosquito-infested marshes. Mosquitoes, of course, carry malaria—which may have convinced the Celts to cross the mountains in search of a better situation.

The arrival of the Celts, undoubtedly, was a cause for concern. The locals had heard of these wild people, a massive network of barbarian tribes scattered all the way from the Atlantic coast to settlements in Asia Minor. Today, we commonly associate the Celts with the Scots, the Irish, the Welsh, and the Cornish, but those people are the remnants of a much larger culture that once dominated most of Europe. The earliest Celtic settlement we have discovered to date is at Hallstatt, Austria, where ancient Celts once mined one of antiquity's most precious commodities: salt.

The modern map of Europe is still dotted with place names that betray ancient Celtic roots. When Julius Caesar eventually marched into what we now call France, he knew it as Gaul, home to a number of fierce Celtic tribes. He wrote that the region was divided into three general areas:

> *The whole of Gaul is divided into three parts, one of which the Belgae inhabit, the Aquitani another, and the third a people who in their own language are called "Celts," but in ours, "Gauls." They all differ among themselves in respect of language, way of life, and laws. The River Garonne divides the Gauls from the Aquitani, and the Marne and Seine rivers separate them from the Belgae. Of these three, the Belgae are the bravest, for they are furthest away from the civilization and culture of the Province. Merchants very rarely travel to them or import such goods as make men's courage weak and womanish.*[1]

Although Julius Caesar divided the inhabitants into separate groups, scholars today believe that the Belgae, while influenced by contact with Germanic tribes, were also Celtic, speaking an early form of their language. The name of the region, *Gaul*, offers an important clue as to where else the Celts may have lived; the syllable "GAL" can be found all over the map: the country of PortuGAL, the religion of GALicia in Spain, the kingdom of GALicia in Poland, and the province of GALatia in Asia Minor. (There is a good chance that Paul's letter to the Galatians was

---

1 Caesar, Julius. Carolyn Hammond, trans. *The Gallic War: Seven Commentaries on The Gallic War with an Eighth Commentary by Aulus Hirtius.* Oxford World's Classics, 2008. Digital, Kindle, 3.

actually addressed to a group of early Celtic believers, although they had likely been thoroughly Hellenized—and subsequently Romanized—by the time Paul wrote.) In northern Italy, where the Celts suddenly appeared, they established a number of cities that persist to this day: Mediolanum (Milan) and Taurinum (Turin).

When the early Greeks and Romans first came in contact with Celtic tribes, they found that these people—known as the *Keltoi* to the Greeks and the *Galli* to the Romans—utterly terrifying. They recognized that there were enough Celts living to the north of them to create serious problems should they suddenly descend on the Mediterranean world.

Diodorus Siculus, the ancient Greek historian, recorded his impressions of the Celts in the middle of the 1st century BC, noting how utterly strange they seemed.

The Gauls are tall of body, with rippling muscles, and white of skin, and their hair is blond, and not only naturally so, but they also make it their practice by artificial means to increase the distinguishing colour which nature has given it. For they are always washing their hair in lime-water, and they pull it back from the forehead to the top of the head and back to the nape of the neck, with the result that their appearance is like that of Satyrs and Pans, since the treatment of their hair makes it so heavy and coarse that it differs in no respect from the mane of horses. Some of them shave the beard, but others let it grow a little; and the nobles shave their cheeks, but they let the moustache grow until it covers the mouth. Consequently, when they are eating, their moustaches become entangled in the food, and when they are drinking, the beverage passes, as it were, through a kind of a strainer. When they dine they all sit, not upon chairs, but upon the ground, using for cushions the skins of wolves or of dogs. The service at the meals is performed by the youngest children, both male and female, who are of suitable age; and near at hand are their fireplaces heaped with coals, and on them are caldrons and spits holding whole pieces of meat. . . .

It is also their custom, when they are formed for battle, to step out in front of the line and to challenge the most valiant men from among their opponents to single combat, brandishing their weapons in front of them to terrify their adversaries. And when any man accepts the challenge to battle, they then break forth into a song in praise of the valiant deeds of their ancestors and in boast of their own high achievements, reviling all the while and belittling their opponent, and trying, in a word, by such talk to strip him of his bold spirit before the combat. When their enemies fall they cut off their heads and fasten them about the necks of their horses; and turning over to their attendants the arms of their opponents, all covered with blood, they carry them off as booty, singing a paean over them and striking up a song of victory, and these first-fruits of battle they fasten by nails upon their houses, just as men do, in certain kinds of hunting, with the heads of wild beasts they have mastered. The heads of their most distinguished enemies they embalm in cedar-oil and carefully preserve in a *chest, and these they exhibit to strangers, gravely maintaining that in exchange for this head some one of their ancestors, or their father, or the man himself, refused the offer of a great sum of money. . . .*

The clothing they wear is striking—shirts which have been dyed and embroidered in varied colours, and breeches, which they call in their tongue bracae; *and they wear striped coats, fastened by a buckle on the shoulder, heavy for winter wear and light for summer, in which are set checks, close together and of varied hues. For armour they use long shields, as high as a man, which are wrought in a manner peculiar to them, some of them even having the figures of animals embossed on them in bronze, and these are skillfully worked with an eye not only to beauty but also to protection. On their heads they put bronze helmets which have large embossed figures standing out from them and give an appearance of great size to those who wear them; for in some cases horns are attached to the helmet so as to form a single piece, in other cases images of the foreparts of birds or four-footed animals. Their trumpets are of peculiar nature and such as barbarians use, for when they are blown upon they give forth a harsh sound, appropriate to the tumult of war. Some of them have iron cuirasses, chain-wrought, but others are satisfied with the armour which Nature has given them and go into battle naked.*[2]

---

2 Siculus, Diodorus. *Complete Works of Diodorus Siculus*. Delphi Ancient Classics, Book 32, 2014. Digital, 6939-6983 on Kindle.

When the Celts arrived in the Po Valley region, the citizens of Clusium were understandably terrified, and sent a message to the Roman Senate, asking for help. Rome was not yet the military powerhouse that it would eventually become, and lacked the resources to provide meaningful military assistance. Instead, they sent three ambassadors to Clusium to broker a peace deal with the Senones, the Celtic tribe that had settled near the city. The Roman historian Livy provides details:

> *The plight of Clusium was a most alarming one: strange men in thousands were at the gates, men the like of whom the townsfolk had never seen, outlandish warriors armed with strange weapons, who were rumoured already to have scattered the Etruscan legions on both sides of the Po; it was a terrible situation, and in spite of the fact that the people of Clusium had no official ties with Rome or reason to expect her friendship, except perhaps that they had refused assistance to their kinsmen of Veii, they sent a mission to ask help from the Senate. Military aid was not granted, but the three sons of Marcus Fabius Ambustus were sent to remonstrate with the Gauls in the Senate's name and to ask them not to molest a people who had done them no wrong and were, moreover, friends and allies of Rome. Rome, they added, would be bound to protect them, even by force, should the need arise, though it would be better, if possible, to avoid recourse to arms and to become acquainted with the new immigrants in a peaceful manner.*[3]

---

3   Livy. *The Early History of Rome: Books 1-5*. Penguin Classics, 2005. Digital, Kindle, 411.

The negotiations went well. The Celts had never heard of the Romans; nevertheless, they were impressed that the delegation had used a diplomatic rather than a military approach, and believed that the Romans must be very influential and powerful if the people of Clusium had appealed to them. They agreed to forgo the conquest of the city in exchange for nearby agricultural land, which was likely all they wanted in the first place. The Roman delegation pushed the issue, pointing out that to demand land in order to avoid war was unethical, and then they questioned the right of the Celts to be in Italy at all.

The Celts replied defiantly, "All things belong to the brave who carry justice on the point of their swords."[4]

The Romans decided to provide assistance to the people of Clusium after all, and in the ensuing scuffle, a member of the delegation killed a prominent Celtic chieftain:

> *Quintus Fabius, riding ahead of the line straight for the Gallic chieftain as he was making for the Etruscan standards, killed him with a spear-thrust through the side and began to strip him of his armour. It was then that the Gauls realized who he was, and word was passed through their ranks that he was the envoy from Rome. At once the trumpets sounded the retreat; the quarrel with Clusium was forgotten and the anger of the barbarian army was turned upon Rome.[5]*

The Celts sent a delegation to Rome and demanded that the family from which the ambassadors had been chosen, the

---

4   Ibid., 412.

5   Ibid.

Fabii, be handed over to them. Rather than handing over the offenders, the Romans promoted them, making them military tribunes for the coming year. The Celts were furious, and threatened the city with war.

In 387 BC, the Celtic warrior Brennus, chieftain of the Senones, marched on the city of Rome. The Roman army met his forces where the River Allia empties into the Tiber, about 11 miles from the city. "The ground in front and on both sides," writes the Roman historian Livy, "was already swarming with enemy soldiers, and the air was loud with the dreadful din of the fierce war-songs and discordant shouts of a people whose very life is wild adventure."[6]

They were roundly beaten by the angry Celts, and made a hasty retreat to the nearby city of Veii. After three days of severing heads from the bodies of their victims, according to custom, the Celts continued their march and discovered a city utterly unprepared for their arrival:

> The Gauls could hardly believe their eyes, so easy, so miraculously swift their victory had been. For a while they stood rooted to the spot, hardly realizing what had happened; then after a moment of fear lest the whole thing were a trap, they began to collect the arms and equipment of the dead and to pile them, as their manner is, in heaps. Finally, when no sign of an enemy was anywhere to be seen, they marched, and shortly before sunset reached the vicinity of Rome. Mounted men were sent forward to reconnoitre: the gates stood open, not a sentry was on guard; no soldiers manned the walls.[7]

---

6   Livy. *The Early History of Rome: Books 1-5*. Penguin Classics, 2005. Digital, Kindle, 413.

7   Ibid., 415.

Most of the Romans, warned by a handful of soldiers who had returned, fled to the safety of a fortress on the Capitoline Hill. The Celts made their way into the city cautiously, amazed at the empty streets and eerie hush that had fallen over Rome. At first, they suspected that it might be a trap, but in time, they realized that the Romans were simply hiding out of sheer terror. Eventually, Brennus and his men made their way into a courtyard where they were greeted by a very strange sight: a group of old bearded men, sitting motionless in chairs.

They were the patricians, the elder statesmen of the city. They had decided against retreating to the Capitoline with the rest, where they would only consume resources that others would need. Instead, they dressed in magisterial purple-hemmed robes, sat in their ivory-lined chairs, and waited for the enemy to arrive. The Celts stopped in their tracks at the sight, uncertain what to make of it:

> . . . *something akin to awe held them back at what met their gaze—those figures seated in the open courtyards, the robes and decorations august beyond reckoning, the majesty expressed in those grave, calm eyes like the majesty of gods. They might have been statues in some holy place, and for a while the Gallic warriors stood entranced; then, on an impulse, one of them touched the beard of a certain Marcus Papirius—it was long, as was the fashion of those days—and the Roman struck him on the head with his ivory staff. That was the beginning: the barbarian flamed into anger and killed him, and the others were butchered where they sat. From that moment no mercy was shown; houses were ransacked and the empty shells set on fire.*[8]

8   Ibid., 418-419.

The siege lasted for seven months. At one point, Brennus' men attempted to covertly scale the hill and surprise the Romans, but the sacred geese of Juno reputedly began honking when they crested the ridge, alerting the Romans to their presence. They were able to successfully fend them off. In time, both sides grew weary, and began to negotiate for peace. The price for Brennus' departure was set: 1,000 pounds of gold.

Where the Romans found such wealth at the end of a lengthy siege remains something of a mystery. As the gold was being weighed, the Romans suspected the Celts of cheating and declared the scales to be rigged. Brennus' quiet reply has become legendary: he threw his sword on the scales and simply said *vae victus*, "woe to the defeated." They paid the price without further complaint.

With that, the Celts left town, carrying what was left of Rome's wealth with them, leaving behind a city determined to never see such humiliation again, and a people who would become intent on conquest. They would ultimately defeat the Celts when Julius Caesar entered Gaul three centuries later.

But the Celts were by no means finished with Rome; 800 years after laying waste to what would eventually be known as the "Eternal City," at about the time Western Roman Empire fell to the Goths, they would displace the city of seven hills in a much more important matter.

CHAPTER TWO:
C. AD 400

IT IS NOT AN EASY TASK TO DETERMINE THE CAUSE of a great historical event, because seldom is one factor enough to explain it. It has been more than 1,500 years since the collapse of the Western Roman Empire, and historians are still debating why it happened. Among the causes usually listed: unsustainable expansion, political corruption, pressure from barbarian raiders, and the shift away from polytheistic paganism to Christianity. The empire was large and remarkably long-lived, so it becomes a formidable task—if not impossible—to determine precisely which factors may have contributed to the fall.

So for the purposes of *this* story, we will simply choose a place to begin: the sudden appearance of the Goths in Roman literature during the 3rd and 4th centuries after Christ. The Goths were a Germanic tribe that originally lived in the region now known as Poland. Over time, they moved southward, into modern-day Ukraine and Romania. By the year AD 250, they were living in settlements on the northwestern shores of the Black Sea and launching raids on the coast of Asia Minor, home to the seven churches mentioned in the book of Revelation.

The Goths, like nearly all raiders of the ancient world, were in the habit of taking captives back with them, and as a result, a number of Christian families suddenly found themselves involuntarily living among barbarians. The Goths did not force them to give up their faith, however, and they were quite happy to share Christ with their captors. Before long, a form of Christianity had taken root among the barbarians who lived just north of the Danube River in Eastern Europe.

Among the descendants of the captives was a man named Ulfilas, which means *little wolf*. His family was taken from a village roughly 50 miles south of modern-day Ankara in Turkey. In spite of his station in life, he was an educated man, fluent in Greek, Latin, and of course the Germanic language of the Goths. How he came to be a man of letters is something of a mystery, since education was generally only available to the wealthy and the aristocrats.

Ulfilas was a Christian. In spite of captivity and servitude, his family had managed to retain their faith and even share it with the Goths. Philostorgius, a historian who lived in Constantinople in the middle of the 4th century, tells us how it happened:

> *[The Goths] made an incursion into the Roman territory, and laid waste a great part of Europe by their predatory excursions and afterwards having crossed over into Asia, invaded Cappadocia and Galatia. Here they took a large quantity of prisoners, among whom were not a few ecclesiastics; and they returned to their own country laden with spoils and booty. These pious captives, by their intercourse with the barbarians, brought over a great number of the latter to the true faith, and persuaded them to embrace the Christian religion in*

place of heathen superstitions. Of the number of these
captives were the ancestors of Ulphilas himself, who
were of Cappadocia descent, deriving their origin from
a village called Sadagolthina, near the city of Parnassus.
This Urphilas, then, was the leader of this pious band
which came out from among the Goths, and became
eventually their first bishop.[9]

In AD 340, at about the age of 30, Ulfilas was sent on an
diplomatic mission to Constantinople, where Constantius II,
Constantine's son, occupied the throne. While there, Ulfilas was
consecrated as a bishop by the patriarch of Constantinople[10] and
sent back to head up a church among the Goths. He took his assignment among the barbarians seriously, developing a written
language for the Goths so that he could translate the Bible for
them. His translation did not include what was known at the
time as the "book of the Kings," however, because of all the military exploits described in them, as he did not wish to encourage
a people he already knew were fond of war.

After about seven years, the king of the Tervingi, the Gothic
tribe that had sent Ulfilas to Constantinople, decided that they
no longer cared for the Christian faith and started persecuting
believers. In response, the bishop to the barbarians uprooted
his community and moved them to safety in Roman territory,
south of the Danube River. The Roman emperor rolled out the

---

9   Philostorgius. *Ecclesiastical History,* Book II, Chapter 5.

10 At this point in history, there were five key centers of influence in
    Christianity: Rome, Jerusalem, Alexandria, Antioch, and Constantinople.
    It was only in later years that Rome was named as *the* center of the official
    Christian church.

welcome mat, giving him land near Nicopolis (in modern-day
Bulgaria), where Ulfilas spent the rest of his life. Constantius II
fondly referred to Ulfilas as the "Moses of our time," because
he had led his group of believers out of captivity into what any
good Roman could only consider the land of promise.

Ulfilas' exodus set an important precedent: the Goths
themselves would soon follow in his footsteps when the Huns
suddenly poured over the Eurasian steppes into their territory.
Nobody is entirely certain where the Huns came from, because
their ancient roots have been obscured by the murk of unwrit-
ten history. Our earliest information dates from the first contact,
when they suddenly appeared in Europe intent on conquest. At
about the time John was writing the book of Revelation, there
were already a number of Huns living near the Caspian Sea; by
the late 4th century, they had expanded alarmingly.

The descriptions of these strange invaders were written by
their enemies, and they are not flattering. Those who saw the
Huns in person describe horrific-looking warriors who had deliberately marred their own facial features in order to inspire
terror. Jordanes, a Goth who wrote about the Huns about a century after their reign of terror ended, described them:

> For by the terror of their features they inspired great fear
> in those whom perhaps they did not really surpass in
> war. They made their foes flee in horror because their
> swarthy aspect was fearful, and they had, if I may call it
> so, a sort of shapeless lump, not a head, with pin-holes
> rather than eyes. Their hardihood is evident in their
> wild appearance, and they are beings who are cruel to
> their children on the very day they are born. For they

cut the cheeks of the males with a sword, so that before they receive the nourishment of milk they must learn to endure wounds. Hence they grow old beardless and their young men are without comeliness, because a face furrowed by the sword spoils by its scars the natural beauty of a beard. They are short in stature, quick in bodily movement, alert horsemen, broad shouldered, ready in the use of bow and arrow, and have firm-set necks which are ever erect in pride. Though they live in the form of men, they have the cruelty of wild beasts.[11]

The wounds inflicted on Hunnic children did not only teach them to endure pain from an early age, but also served to make them appear more ferocious on the battlefield. And even though they did not have advanced metallurgy, as expert horsemen and capable archers, they were a force to be reckoned with. A rumor began to spread among the Goths that the Huns must be descended from witches. King Filimer, the story was told, had cast the witches out of Gothic territory in the distant past. They made their way to the remote steppes, where they had illicit relations with evil spirits and gave birth to a race of half-man, half-monster warriors. They had now come to take vengeance on Filimer's people.

The Goths were terrified and began to flee southward, toward the Danube River—the northern border of the Roman Empire. Thousands of desperate refugees piled up against the river, hoping to cross into the safety of the Roman Empire. Emperor Valens, who now ruled in Constantinople, granted them

---

11   Jordanes. *The Goths*, XXIV. Princeton: Theophania Publishing, 1915, 48.

permission, just as Constantius had given asylum to Ulfilas years earlier. The Goths crossed the river and moved into Roman holding camps on the south shore.

The emperor sent emergency rations to support the migrants, but two of his Roman commanders saw the shipment of supplies as an opportunity for profit. Instead of distributing the goods, they began to sell them. When both the imperial supplies and the Goths' money began to run low, the price of food skyrocketed, and the Goths were eventually offered dog meat if they would surrender their children to become Roman slaves.

Driven by desperation, the angry Goths pushed back. They had been promised farmland; instead, they were facing starvation. Following the lead of their king, Fritigern, they started to loot and pillage the neighboring countryside, taking whatever they wanted to sustain themselves. Valens was left with little choice but to respond with force; he brought an army of 30,000 Roman troops to the region in order to quash the Gothic rebellion.

In AD 378, Valens met the desperate barbarians just outside of the city of Adrianople, located on the northwestern corner of modern-day Turkey. It should have been an easy win for the Romans, but it proved to be perhaps the greatest blow ever dealt to the empire. The Romans were utterly humiliated on the battlefield. The emperor's body was never found.

The shock spread across the ancient world. The Goths' victory signaled a decisive turning point in Roman fortunes. Toward the end of the 3rd century, Diocletian had brought stability to the Roman Empire with his *tetrarchy*, a system that placed two rulers—a senior *Augustus* and a junior *Caesar*—in each half of the empire. His brutality ensured that threats were minimized. Constantine the Great went one step further, uniting the entire empire under himself. Barbarian invasions and civil war seemed to be a thing of the past, and Rome was the most stable it had been in many generations.

The humiliating defeat at the Battle of Adrianople changed all that, and today, many historians pinpoint the year AD 378 as the beginning of the end for the western half of the Roman Empire. A further blow was dealt to the Romans two years later when Gothic forces defeated Theodosius, the last emperor to rule over both halves of the empire, in Macedonia. Rome was learning that they would have to negotiate with the Goths, because they could not defeat them.

The Goths settled in the Balkans, and in AD 382, Fritigern died. He was replaced by Alaric, a Goth whose name has become synonymous with Roman defeat. Alaric and his men started pushing into Greek territory, and by the turn of the century, they made their way into Italy. The western emperor, Honorius, was horrified, and quickly moved his administrative capital from Milan to Ravenna, which he believed could be more easily defended. For a time, the Roman general Stilicho managed to ward off the Goths, but when the emperor suspected him of fraternizing with the barbarians, he was summarily executed, and Alaric was able to push deep into Italian territory.

Less than 100 years after Constantine rode into Rome with the head of Maxentius on a spear, the citizens of the Eternal City suddenly awoke to literal barbarians at the gate. Alaric and his men arrived outside of Rome in AD 408. Nervous Romans became convinced that the Goths had been sent by jilted pagan gods who had been neglected since the Christianization of the empire under Constantine. In order to appease the gods, it was suggested that ancient pagan rituals be reinstated. Innocent I, the Bishop of Rome, agreed to allow it, provided that the sacrifices be done in secret. The pagan priests refused, insisting that the only appropriate thing to do would be to honor the gods publicly, in the Roman Forum. Anything less would be further insult.

The sacrifices never took place.

Over the next couple of years, Alaric waged three separate sieges on the city. The first one was stopped when the Roman Senate paid him to bring it to an end. There was a second siege in AD 409, and finally, on August 24, AD 410, Alaric caught a lucky break: rebellious slaves inside the city, tired of their Roman masters, opened the Salarian Gate for Alaric and allowed the Goths to pour into the city. The invaders immediately set fire to all the nearby homes and started ransacking the rest of the city.

The Romans pled with Alaric to stop, asking what it would take to make him go away. He demanded all of the valuables of the city and the release of every barbarian slave. When a prominent Roman protested, asking what the citizens would be left with, Alaric replied, "Your lives."

The victorious Goths were so weighed down with the spoils of war on their way out of town that those who were present recorded that they had to move very slowly. The great city was left desolate, completely stripped of its wealth. And yet many of the buildings were spared, and according to some accounts, the Goths actually refused to take any objects that appeared to be Christian. Many of them were, after all, Christians themselves, disciples of Ulfilas. The story is told that when Alaric's men discovered gold and silver items that had supposedly belonged to the Apostle Peter, they refused to take them, but delivered them safely to St. Peter's Church instead.

In the wake of heart-wrenching defeat, pagan Romans continued to point the finger at Christians, insisting that the change of religion brought to the empire by Constantine had led directly to the sack of the city. Augustine of Hippo, the famous North African theologian, disagreed. Instead of blaming Christians, he said, the pagans should *thank* them: it was Alaric's respect for Christianity that had stopped the devastation from getting worse. Had they not noticed that even pagans were able to find refuge in Christian churches?

> *Are not those very Romans, who were spared by the barbarians through their respect for Christ, become enemies to the name of Christ? The reliquaries of the martyrs and the churches of the apostles bear witness to this; for in the sack of the city they were open sanctuary for all who fled to them, whether Christian or Pagan. To their very threshold the blood-thirsty enemy raged; there his murderous fury owned a limit. Thither did such of the enemy as had any pity convey those to whom they had given quarter, lest any less mercifully disposed might fall upon them. And, indeed, when even those murderers who everywhere else showed themselves pitiless came to those spots where that was forbidden which the license of war permitted in every other place, their furious rage for slaughter was bridled, and their eagerness to take prisoners was quenched. Thus escaped multitudes who now reproach the Christian religion, and impute to Christ the ills that have befallen their city; but the preservation of their own life—a boon which they owe to the respect entertained*

for Christ by the barbarians—they attribute not to our Christ, but to their own good luck.[12]

News from Adrianople had troubled the Roman world; the news that Rome had fallen shook it to the core. Jerome, the man who gave us the Vulgate Bible, heard of Rome's defeat from his home in Bethlehem. "My voice sticks in my throat," he wrote, "and, as I dictate, sobs choke my utterance. The City which had taken the world was itself taken."[13]

Theodosius II, the emperor in Constantinople, called for three days of mourning.

In the west, it was over. On September 4, AD 476, another Germanic barbarian, Odoacer, removed the last Western emperor from his throne. Romulus Augustus offered such little resistance that Odoacer spared his life and sent him off into peaceful retirement. Odoacer became the first barbarian king of Italy. Less than a thousand years after the first—and only other—siege on Rome, the Western Empire was finished.

12　Augustine of Hippo. *The City of God,* Book I, Sec. 1. New York: Modern Library Edition, 1993, 4.

13　Jerome. *Letter CXXVII (To Principia).*

CHAPTER THREE:
C. 600 BC

CONSTANTIUS II HAD REFERRED TO ULFILAS AS the "Moses of our time," noting how he had led an exodus of barbarian Christians into the safety of Roman territory. There is another appropriate biblical title for Ulfilas: the Daniel of his time. He was, after all, the son of captives who managed to bring the faith of Abraham to a heathen, idol-worshipping land.

About 150 years after the city of Rome was originally founded,[14] a king from another land suddenly woke up in the middle of the night, his sleep disturbed by a troubling dream. His name was Nebuchadnezzar, potentate of the Neo-Babylonian Empire. His mind was so agitated that he could not return to sleep, so he summoned his most trusted advisors, the Chaldeans.

When they arrived, Nebuchadnezzar asked them to explain what he had seen:

> *Then the king gave the command to call the magicians, the astrologers, the sorcerers, and the Chaldeans to tell the king his dreams. So they came and stood before the king. And the king said to them, "I have had a dream, and my spirit is anxious to know the dream." Then the*

---

14 Legend has it that Rome was founded by Romulus and Remus on August 21, 753 BC.

Chaldeans spoke to the king in Aramaic, "O king, live forever! Tell your servants the dream, and we will give the interpretation." (Daniel 2:2-4)

It should have been a rather straightforward assignment. In ancient Mesopotamia, dreams were regarded as highly significant—a probable message from the gods. Archeology has unearthed massive collections of dream interpretation books, indicating that the royal counselors of the ancient world were likely well-prepared to explain what Nebuchadnezzar had seen. All they needed was the content of the dream.

On the night in question, they were presented with an unusual challenge. The king refused to reveal what he had seen, perhaps prompted by the dream itself to become suspicious of his counselors' ability to communicate with the gods. "You're not just going to tell me what the dream means," he told them, "I want you to tell me what I dreamt. If you can't, I will have you dismembered!" (Daniel 2:5)

It was, of course, the impossible task, and a command was issued to round up every last Chaldean and put them all to death. As the army went through the city, they came to the house of a young Hebrew captive named Daniel, likely less than 20 years old at the time. He was a member of the royal family, placed in a special training program by Nebuchadnezzar in order to inculcate him with Babylonian values. If Hebrew leadership learned to think and act like Babylonians, then the rest of the people would follow suit, and the risk of an uprising would be drastically curtailed.

Daniel, it turns out, proved to be wiser than the king's own men, and even though he resisted Babylonian religion and culture, he was placed among the king's counselors. Unfortunately for him, that meant being swept up in the pogrom against the Chaldeans. When he discovered the cause of the crisis, he asked to be taken to Nebuchadnezzar:

> *So the decree went out, and they began killing the wise men; and they sought Daniel and his companions, to kill them. Then with counsel and wisdom Daniel answered Arioch, the captain of the king's guard, who had gone out to kill the wise men of Babylon; he answered and said to Arioch the king's captain, "Why is the decree from the king so urgent?" Then Arioch made the decision known to Daniel. So Daniel went in and asked the king to give him time, that he might tell the king the interpretation.* (Daniel 2:13-16)

He was granted the time he requested, and instead of running over to the Chaldean library for advice, he gathered three of his friends, also young Hebrew captives, and made the king's dream a matter of prayer. In the middle of the night, Daniel was shown what the king had seen.

The next day, he was ushered into Nebuchadnezzar's presence, where he described the dream in detail:

> *"You, O king, were watching; and behold, a great image! This great image, whose splendor was excellent, stood before you; and its form was awesome. This image's head was of fine gold, its chest and arms of silver, its belly and thighs of bronze, its legs of iron, its feet partly of iron and partly of clay. You watched while a stone*

was cut out without hands, which struck the image on its feet of iron and clay, and broke them in pieces. Then the iron, the clay, the bronze, the silver, and the gold were crushed together, and became like chaff from the summer threshing floors; the wind carried them away so that no trace of them was found. And the stone that struck the image became a great mountain and filled the whole earth. This is the dream. Now we will tell the interpretation of it before the king." (Daniel 2:31-36)

To have someone accurately describe a statue you saw in a dream would a powerful attention-getter. Of course, at this point, it is just an old story, and skeptics find it easy to explain it away: ancient history is replete with miracle stories, and without having been there, we can neither confirm nor deny that it actually happened. And, given the impossibility of the story, skeptics are happy to declare that it didn't.

What is not so easy to account for, however, is the explanation Daniel gives. The statue, he goes on to tell the king, predicts the rise and fall of large empires:

"You, O king, are a king of kings. For the God of heaven has given you a kingdom, power, strength, and glory; and wherever the children of men dwell, or the beasts of the field and the birds of the heaven, He has given them into your hand, and has made you ruler over them all—you are this head of gold. But after you shall arise another kingdom inferior to yours; then another, a third kingdom of bronze, which shall rule over all the earth. And the fourth kingdom shall be as

strong as iron, inasmuch as iron breaks in pieces and shatters everything; and like iron that crushes, that kingdom will break in pieces and crush all the others."
(Daniel 2:37-40)

The prediction is breathtaking. The statue's golden head, Daniel explains, represents Nebuchadnezzar and the Babylonian Empire that God allowed him to have. It would eventually be replaced by another empire, represented by the chest and arms of silver. That is precisely what happened, when Cyrus the Persian general sacked the city of Babylon in 539 BC, propelling the Medes and the Persians to the apex of power in the ancient world.

In AD 331, the Persians were displaced by the "belly and thighs of bronze" when Alexander the Great defeated them at the Battle of Arbela, giving rise to the Hellenistic period, when the Greeks ruled the world. Alexander was ambitious—expanding his territory as far as India—and it is because of Greek domination that the New Testament was written in Alexander's language, even though by then, the Romans had risen to power.

The iron legs pointed to a fourth empire, the Romans, who upset the Macedonians in 168 BC at the Battle of Pydna. From that point forward, the Roman Empire came into its own, and would last—at least in the west—until Ocoacer removed Romulus Augustus from the throne in AD 476.

It is not a great feat to suggest that the future would produce a string of successive empires; anybody familiar with history—as the learned Daniel would have been—could make such a prediction. It would be akin to predicting that the might of the 19th-century British Empire would eventually fade away; it is a reasonable, educated guess. There are a couple of factors, however, that remove Nebuchadnezzar's dream from the realm of guesswork.

First, the rest of the book of Daniel goes into astounding detail, going so far as to list both the Persians and the Greeks by name in a parallel prediction in the 8th chapter. The accuracy and the level of detail provided in chapters 7, 8, and 11 are so compelling that it has led some skeptics to surmise—wrongly— that it must have been written after the fact.

The second factor is the number of empires predicted. The dream did not anticipate five empires, or three, but precisely the correct number: *four*. There would not be a fifth:

> *"Whereas you saw the feet and toes, partly of potter's clay and partly of iron, the kingdom shall be divided; yet the strength of the iron shall be in it, just as you saw the iron mixed with ceramic clay. And as the toes of the feet were partly of iron and partly of clay, so the kingdom shall be partly strong and partly fragile. As you saw iron mixed with ceramic clay, they will mingle with the seed of men; but they will not adhere to one another, just as iron does not mix with clay."* (Daniel 2:41-43)

The legs of iron, representing the Roman Empire, would not give rise to another broad-based, unified kingdom. Instead, the dream predicted dissolution and fragmentation. The iron legs end with 10 toes. There would be something left of Rome's iron, but it would be mixed with clay, and the broken empire would never be reassembled into a single political entity.

That is precisely what happened with the Western Roman Empire. After AD 476, it shattered into a collection of barbarian kingdoms, many of which remain with us to this day in the form of European nations: the Franks, the Alemanni, the Lombards, the Anglo-Saxons, and so on. To date, every attempt to reassemble the empire has failed, exactly as Daniel said would happen. It is a state of affairs, according to Daniel 2, that will last until God Himself establishes a kingdom on earth.

The arrival of angry Goths at the gates of the eternal city in AD 410 may have come as a surprise to the Romans, but it would not have been a surprise to a young Hebrew captive who saw it a thousand years before it happened.

CHAPTER FOUR:
A PALE HORSE RIDES

THE FOUR HORSEMEN OF THE APOCALYPSE, FOUND in the 6th chapter of Revelation, have provided rich fodder for apocalyptic writing in modern times. They are usually associated with the end of time—each horse assigned a particular function in earth's final crisis. The following passage, taken from a book on Bible prophecy by best-selling authors Tim La-Haye and Jerry B. Jenkins, is a good representation of modern thought on the subject:

> The many plagues of the Tribulation will be so extensive that only a small percent of the world's population will remain by the time Christ returns. Considering together the Rapture, the four horsemen of the Apocalypse, the many judgments of God, and the martyrdom of the saints during the second half of the Tribulation, it is unlikely that half a billion people will still be living on the planet when Jesus Christ returns. Probably billions will die of the plagues. Others will die from wars, earthquakes, changes in nature, and the other judgments of God. Unsanitary conditions

will be everywhere during that time, doubtlessly exacerbating the many infectious diseases that already will be out of control.[15]

The authors go on to explain that the first (white) horse represents the Antichrist, who succeeds in crowning himself over the nations of earth. The second (red) horse points to a massive world war that takes place when kingly forces dare to oppose the Antichrist. The third (black) horse predicts rampant inflation and economic collapse taking place in the wake of war, leading to worldwide death, disease, and famine. The fourth (pale) horse is the most ominous of all, prophesying widespread death that follows the first three horses.

It is not unlike other modern interpretations, such as the one provided in Hal Lindsey's runaway best-seller of the 1970s, *The Late, Great Planet Earth*:

Almost immediately after the Antichrist declares himself to be God, God releases the dreaded second of the four horsemen of the Apocalypse. This is a figure of the unleashing of war upon the earth. That beautiful balance of power established by the Antichrist is suddenly ruptured. God begins to show man that the Antichrist's promises cannot stand. The thing which man feared most, an all-out war, now rushes upon him.[16]

15 LaHaye, Tim and Jerry B. Jenkins. *Are We Living in the End Times?* Wheaton: Tyndale House, 1999, 179.

16 Lindsey, Hal. *The Late, Great Planet Earth*. Zondervan, 1970. Digital, 2357-2361 on Kindle.

This style of interpreting the four horsemen—as horrific events that take place in a final tribulation period—has been the predominant method used by Western Christians in the 20th and early 21st century. Authors have attempted to find evidence that the horsemen have begun to ride in almost every major geopolitical event of the last century, ranging from the rebirth of Israel in 1948 to the tensions of the Cold War to Barack Obama's presidency.

It is now such a widely-held interpretation that it comes as a surprise to many Christians to discover that it is a very recent one. Before the 19th century, our forefathers in the Christian faith wouldn't have recognized the way we now talk about the 6th chapter of Revelation. To them, the seven seals (of which the horsemen are the first four) were historical in nature, describing the unbroken history of the Christian church from its earliest, apostolic days to the *parousia,* the glorious return of Christ. They understood the four horses as covering a story that unfolded over centuries, not mere years.

Such was the case with Victorinus of Pettau in Pannonia, a scholar who died less than 10 years before Constantine won the Battle of the Milvian Bridge in AD 312. He noticed that each set of seven in the Apocalypse—seven churches, seven seals, seven trumpets—seemed to be parallel prophecies that covered similar ground: the complete span of Christian history.

Along with other early church fathers, he also saw the "son of perdition" mentioned in Paul's second letter to the Thessalonians as a figure who would emerge once the all-powerful Roman Empire was no longer standing in the way. "For the mystery of lawlessness is already at work," Paul wrote, "only he who now restrains will do so until he is taken out of the way."

The "he" was almost universally understood to be the Roman Empire.

Victorinus, of course, died more than a century before Alaric marched into the city of Rome and guaranteed its demise, but it should be noted that early Christian believers understood from the prophetic books of the Bible that Rome would eventually fall. Writing toward the end of the 2nd century, Tertullian explained:

> "For the mystery of iniquity doth already work; only he who now hinders must hinder, until he be taken out of the way." What obstacle is there but the Roman state, the falling away of which, by being scattered into ten kingdoms, shall introduce Antichrist upon (its own ruins)? "And then shall be revealed the wicked one, whom the Lord shall consume with the spirit of His mouth, and shall destroy with the brightness of His coming: even him whose coming is after the working of Satan, with all power, and signs, and lying wonders, and with all deceivableness of unrighteousness in them that perish."[17]

Augustine, who was alive during Alaric's sack of Rome, and who could hear barbarians attacking his own North African city years later as he lay on his deathbed, agreed:

> Some think that the Apostle Paul referred to the Roman empire, and that he was unwilling to use language more explicit, lest he should incur the calumnious

---

17 Tertullian. *The Complete Works of Tertullian* (33 Books With Active Table of Contents). Digital, 23359-23364 on Kindle.

charge of wishing ill to the empire which it was hoped
would be eternal; so that in saying, "For the mystery of
iniquity doth already work," he alluded to Nero, whose
deeds already seemed to be as the deeds of Antichrist.
And hence some suppose that he shall rise again and
be Antichrist. Others, again, suppose that he is not
even dead, but that he was concealed that he might
be supposed to have been killed, and that he now lived
in concealment in the vigor of that same age which he
had reached when he was believed to have perished,
and will live until he is revealed in his own time and
restored to his kingdom. But I wonder that men can
be so audacious in their conjectures. However, it is not
absurd to believe that these words of the apostle, "Only
he who now holdeth, let him hold until he be taken out
of the way," refer to the Roman Empire, as if it were
said, "Only he who now reigneth, let him reign until he
be taken out of the way."[18]

Armed with the knowledge that Daniel had successfully
predicted the progression of world empires from Babylon to the
fragmentation of the Roman Empire, the early church viewed
Bible prophecy as a continually unfolding process that began in
the day of the prophet and moved forward to the *eschaton*, the
end of the world. They saw the same pattern in John's prophecies: they were continuous, historical prophecies that would
unfold across many generations.

---

18   Augustine of Hippo, *The City of God*. Book XX, Sec. 19. New York:
      Modern Library Edition, 1993, 739.

It is an understanding that is easily derived from the text of Revelation itself. At the opening of the book, John is told that he will witness "things which must shortly take place." (Revelation 1:1)

Events scheduled 2,000 years into the future cannot be said to take place *shortly*; it is only in very recent times that most Christians have begun to interpret most of Revelation as something that was written for a far-off future generation. The original readers of the book understood that the events of Revelation began to unfold as soon as John received it.

To this day, Bible students still recognize that the seven churches described at the beginning of Revelation correspond to seven periods of Christian history, perhaps the last remaining portion of Revelation to still be understood this way:

1) **The Church of Ephesus** points to the early apostolic church in its original purity. It was in danger of becoming lackadaisical, and losing its first love.

2) **The Church of Smyrna** predicted a church that would be relentlessly persecuted by the pagan Roman Empire.

3) **The Church of Pergamos** predicted a compromise that took place after the supposed conversion of the Emperor Constantine, who brought a sudden halt to persecution and endorsed Christianity to the point where it quickly became the official religion of the Western Roman Empire.[19]

---

19 The prequel to this volume, *Shadow Emperor*, describes this fascinating moment in Christian history in some detail.

4) **The Church of Thyatira** predicted the church of the Dark Ages, which lost most of its mission-driven fervor after blending Christian faith with Roman politics. As the Western Roman Empire collapsed, and the center of political power retreated to Constantinople in the east, Christian clergy filled the power vacuum left behind, and allowed political power and conquest to overshadow the Gospel Commission given to the church by Christ.

5) **The Church of Sardis** predicted a moment in Christian history when the tide began to turn, and voices in the late Middle Ages began to call for dramatic reform—voices like those of Tyndale, Huss, and Luther.

6) **The Church of Philadelphia** predicted a revitalization of Christianity after the close of the Dark Ages. This was the period during which the Bible and missionary societies were founded, and it was marked by great Christian revivals across the Western world, often referred to as the First and Second Great Awakenings.

7) **The Church of Laodicea,** tragically, predicts a last-day generation of Christians whose faith is tepid and weak.

You will notice that most modern translations of the Bible that use subtitles in the text assign each of the seven churches a title that roughly corresponds with this brief outline, reflecting our long-held historical approach to Bible prophecy. In most editions of the New King James Version, for example, the letter to Smyrna has been labeled "The Persecuted Church," the letter to Pergamos has been labeled "The Compromising Church," and so on.

For long centuries, we interpreted the seven seals of Revelation chapter 6 the same way, as historical in nature. The number *seven*, in Bible prophecy, denotes perfection and/or completion. The seven churches are a complete history of Christianity, and historically, Christians would have expected the same from the seven seals: a complete historical description.[20]

Viewing the horsemen of the Apocalypse as historical epochs of Christianity, the way our ancient forefathers did, yields exceptionally interesting results:

1. The White Horse

> *Now I saw when the Lamb opened one of the seals; and I heard one of the four living creatures saying with a voice like thunder, "Come and see." And I looked, and behold, a white horse. He who sat on it had a bow; and a crown was given to him, and he went out conquering and to conquer. (Revelation 6:1, 2)*

In the book of Revelation, the color *white* is a significant symbol, appearing many times:

Ch.	Element
1	Jesus appears to John with hair as white as wool.
2	The faithful are promised a white stone.
3	The faithful are shown wearing white garments.

---

20 The author has detailed why Christians recently altered their approach to prophecy in the book *The Appearing*.

Ch.	Element *(cont.)*
4	The elders in heaven are dressed in white.
6	The martyrs are given white robes to wear.
7	The numberless crowd of the saved is dressed in white.
14	Jesus returns to earth on a white cloud.
19	Jesus returns to earth riding a white horse.
20	God is seated on a white throne during the judgment of the dead.

White, in the ancient world, was a symbol of purity, as it still is today:

> *"Come now, and let us reason together," says the Lord,
> "Though your sins are like scarlet, they shall be as white
> as snow; though they are red like crimson, they shall be
> as wool."* (Isaiah 1:18)

The white horse is a picture of the 1st-century apostolic church, a generation of Christians who were clear about the task Jesus had left to them: make disciples of all nations. Among them were people who had personally spoken to Christ. They had heard Him preach, watched Him heal, witnessed His grisly death on a Roman cross, and most importantly, they had seen Him back from the dead. "He was seen by over five hundred brethren at once," Paul wrote to the believers in Corinth. (1 Corinthians 15:6)

Armed with a gospel message direct from the mouth of Jesus Himself, there was no stopping these earliest Christians. They were so passionate about Jesus that they came to be known as the ones "who have turned the world upside down." (Acts 17:6) The risen Christ had told them to carry the news to the "end of the earth" (Acts 1:8)—a commission they took seriously.

Their passion for the work of the church was unrivaled, even to this day, as author Michael Green points out in the introduction to his history of 1st-century evangelism:

> One of the most notable impressions the literature of the first and second century made upon me as I wrote this book was the sheer passion of these early Christians. They were passionately convinced of the truth of the gospel. They were persuaded that men and women were lost without it. They shared in God's own love, poured out on a needy world. They paid heed to Christ's Great Commission. They sought to interpenetrate society with the gospel which had had so profound an effect on them. Christianity for them was no hour's slot on a Sunday. It affected everything they did and everyone they met. Their church life was warm and nourishing, for the most part, and equipped people to move out with the good news. The ordinary Christians, the missionaries, the academics, the women, all seem to have shared in this same passionate commitment to the cause. It was rather like the early communists—small groups bound together by an overmastering passion. Or like the Maquis in the Second World War, secret groups of men who would stop at nothing in order to bring the final day of victory nearer. I do not see much of that spirit in modern churches in the West, though it is a major characteristic of the overflowing churches in Africa, Asia, and Latin America. But without it, how will anyone in our jaded society be moved? They may be pardoned for reflecting,

"These people are Christians, are they? Very nice for them, if they like that sort of thing. But it has nothing to offer me." Not until we burn with a passion, which is almost a pain, to reach people with the gospel, will they be likely to take the matter seriously.[21]

The wild success of the early Christian church was unlikely. The first believers were uneducated and hardly influential. The Jewish nation was considered insignificant by the Romans—a mediocre province on the edge of the empire. And yet, by the time a single generation of believers had passed, Paul was able to write that the gospel had been preached to "every creature under heaven." (Colossians 1:23) Without the benefit of email, social media, or television, the disciples managed to carry the message of a risen Christ to the whole of the Roman Empire.

And so the early church is depicted as a rider on a white horse, armed with a bow and wearing a crown. It was a conquering church, virtually unstoppable in its efforts to bring Christ to the world and the world to Christ. In the beginning, the Romans paid Christians little heed, considering them to be an obscure sect of Jews. But as the division between Jew and Christian deepened, and Jewish synagogues made an effort to distance themselves from the followers of the Nazarene, Rome began to pay more attention.

These "Christians," as they were first called in the city of Antioch (Acts 11:26), worshipped the King of kings, and refused to bow the knee to any other god. The Romans were a remarkably tolerant empire—allowing subjugated nations to keep their reli-

---

21   Green, Michael. *Evangelism in the Early Church.* Surrey: Hodder and Stoughton, 1970, xiii.

gious rituals intact, with only one proviso: they had to add Caesar to their list of gods. In reality, very few Romans actually believed that the emperor was divine; many of them, after all, had grown up with the man and were well aware of his faults. The emperor was, to the Romans, a symbol of national unity, and as such, was considered the embodiment of *Roma,* the goddess of Rome.

To worship the emperor was to pledge allegiance to the empire—nothing more, nothing less. But even a symbolic god was impermissible to the Christians, so the wrath of Rome eventually fell on them, and the white horse of victory suddenly gave way to the red horse of persecution.

2. The Red Horse

> *When He opened the second seal, I heard the second living creature saying, "Come and see." Another horse, fiery red, went out. And it was granted to the one who sat on it to take peace from the earth, and that people should kill one another; and there was given to him a great sword.* (Revelation 6:3, 4)

As Christians began to permeate the Roman Empire, their presence was noted and popular opinion turned against them. They were suspected of sedition—of trying to undermine the empire. They spoke of a world that would end in flames when the King of kings returned to overthrow all human kingdoms—a prospect that did not thrill the powerful Romans.

In time, anti-Christian pamphlets were circulated, and Christians were accused of unthinkable atrocities like incest and cannibalism. In reality, these accusations were distortions of Christian teaching and practice. They were accused of incest because they attended *agape* or "love" feasts, which they attended with men and women they referred to as "brothers and sisters." In reality, these were simply communion services, but gossiping tongues seldom care about the truth. Christians were also accused of cannibalism because of the communion service, where they spoke of "eating the body" and "drinking the blood."

The story of how Christians fell out of favor has been covered extensively in another book (*Shadow Emperor*), so we will not repeat it in detail here. Suffice it to say that when Rome decided she did not like Christians, things took a turn for the worse. They were accused of having burned down the city of Rome, when in reality, Nero had set the fire. They were thrown to wild animals for sport. They were dipped in tar, crucified, and set afire to serve as night lights. It was the most trying period of Christian history, culminating with an especially fierce 10-year persecution launched by the Emperor Diocletian, spanning the years from AD 303-313.[22]

Red, historically, has been the color of blood, warfare, and violence. In the same passage where God pleads with Israel to repent and become "white as snow" (Isaiah 1:18), He points out that without forgiveness, their sins are "like scarlet." Their sins are red, the color of death, for the "wages of sin is death." (Romans 6:23) The relative peace enjoyed by the early Christian church disappeared as the wrath of the Roman Empire turned against her.

In another passage from Revelation, found in the 12th chapter, the same violent eventuality is predicted in a stunning drama that involves a dragon, a baby, and a woman:

---

22 As explained in *Shadow Emperor,* this 10-year persecution is prefigured as a 10-day period of tribulation in Revelation's letter to Smyrna. (See Revelation 2:10.)

Now a great sign appeared in heaven: a woman clothed with the sun, with the moon under her feet, and on her head a garland of twelve stars. Then being with child, she cried out in labor and in pain to give birth. (Revelation 12:1, 2)

In the language of prophecy, a *woman* is often used to represent the people of God. In the 16th chapter of Ezekiel, for example, Israel is portrayed as a baby girl who has been left in the wilderness to die. God finds her, cleans her up, raises her, and she becomes His bride—His covenant people. In the New Testament, Jesus describes the Second Coming as the return of a bridegroom (Matthew 25:1-13), and Paul speaks of having betrothed the Corinthian church to Christ. (2 Corinthians 11:2) Even more directly, Paul compares marriage itself to the relationship between Jesus and the church. (Ephesians 5:30-32)

In Revelation, God's people are portrayed as a woman waiting for the birth of the Messiah. She is clothed with the sun—a direct source of light, and has the moon as her foundation—a source of reflected light. To early Christians, this represented the direct revelation of Christ found in the New Testament, and the reflected light of Christ found in the Old Testament. As John watches, a red dragon enters the scene:

And another sign appeared in heaven: behold, a great, fiery red dragon having seven heads and ten horns, and seven diadems on his heads. His tail drew a third of the stars of heaven and threw them to the earth. And the dragon stood before the woman who was ready to give birth, to devour her Child as soon as it was born. (Revelation 12:3, 4)

The heads and horns, as we will see in another chapter, are reminiscent of the four worldly empires mentioned in the book of Daniel. The dragon, who is said to be Satan (Revelation 12:9), is shown working through the kingdoms of men to destroy the Child the moment He is born. This, of course, proved to be absolutely true: Herod, an agent of the Roman Empire, was threatened by the news that the long-awaited King had been born, and he attempted to destroy the Messiah by murdering every child in his realm. (Matthew 2:16)

It was, of course, a failed attempt. The One who would eventually replace all worldly kingdoms with an eternal kingdom of His own was born, crucified, rose from the dead, and returned to His Father's throne in heaven:

> She bore a male Child who was to rule all nations with
> a rod of iron. And her Child was caught up to God and
> His throne. (Revelation 12:5)

At this juncture, the woman is said to flee to the wilderness, a key point that we will take up again shortly. Later on in the chapter, when the dragon realizes that he has been defeated by Christ's victory at the cross, he turns his wrath against the Christian church:

> "Therefore rejoice, O heavens, and you who dwell in
> them! Woe to the inhabitants of the earth and the sea!
> For the devil has come down to you, having great wrath,
> because he knows that he has a short time." Now when
> the dragon saw that he had been cast to the earth, he
> persecuted the woman who gave birth to the male Child.
> (Revelation 12:12, 13)

Unable to defeat Jesus, the dragon next turned his wrath against the apple of God's eye: the church, the bride of Christ. A pagan empire, predicted among the empires of Daniel, attempted to destroy the church. John penned the book of Revelation toward the end of the 1st century, when Roman toleration of Christians was already drawing to a close, and they were beginning to feel the wrath of the empire. John himself was a prisoner of faith, exiled to the tiny island of Patmos for the perceived threat he posed to the Romans, and for refusing to renounce his faith, and he was the only one of the 12 disciples to escape a martyr's death:

> The "beloved disciple," was brother to James the Great. The churches of Smyrna, Pergamos, Sardis, Philadelphia, Laodicea, and Thyatira, were founded by him. From Ephesus he was ordered to be sent to Rome, where it is affirmed he was cast into a cauldron of boiling oil. He escaped by miracle, without injury. Domitian afterwards banished him to the Isle of Patmos, where he wrote the Book of Revelation. Nerva, the successor of Domitian, recalled him. He was the only apostle who escaped a violent death.[23]

The book of Revelation is pregnant with warning: the road ahead would not be easy for Christians. Those present at the Council of Nicaea (AD 325), which sat shortly after the persecution ended, recorded that every single delegate was maimed in some way. Few escaped the wrath of Rome. Fortunately, the

---

23   Foxe, John. *Foxe's Book of Martyrs.* Digital, 149-153 on Kindle.

period of the red horse, spanning from approximately the close of the 1st century to the beginning of the 4th, eventually came to an end.

3. The Black Horse

When He opened the third seal, I heard the third living creature say, "Come and see." So I looked, and behold, a black horse, and he who sat on it had a pair of scales in his hand. And I heard a voice in the midst of the four living creatures saying, "A quart of wheat for a denarius, and three quarts of barley for a denarius; and do not harm the oil and the wine." (Revelation 6:5, 6)

When the Emperor Diocletian, responsible for the 10-year persecution launched in AD 303, finally retired from public office in AD 305, he left behind a *tetrarchy.* Power was not centered in a single individual, but rather spread across four men. There were two rulers in the west, and two in the east: a senior *Augustus,* and a junior *Caesar.* In the process of choosing his rulers, however, Diocletian passed over Maxentius—the son of Maximian (his former Augustus in the west), and son-in-law to his Caesar in the east, Galerius. Unhappy with having been overlooked, Maxentius approached the Roman Senate, which had long ago ceased to be a center of influence for the empire, and convinced them that by declaring him to be emperor, their former glory could be restored.

With Maxentius in Rome, the empire now had *five* emperors, and before long, Constantine marched on the Eternal City to put a stop to his claims. In October of AD 312, Constantine won a decisive victory at the Battle of the Milvian Bridge, and soon thereafter became the sole ruler of the entire empire. It was one of the most important turning points in Western history: Constantine, his own mother having become a Christian some years earlier, was sympathetic to the Christian faith. While he himself did not submit to baptism until many years later, he put an official stop to the persecution of the church with the Edict of Milan in AD 313, precisely 10 years after it began. Lands and buildings that had been confiscated were returned to the church, and Miltiades, the Bishop of Rome, was given the magnificent Lateran Palace as his new home.

Ten years after his conquest of the city, at a celebration for his decade of rule, Constantine suddenly attributed his victory to the Christian God, insisting that he had seen a vision of the cross in the sky, and heard a voice telling him, *In hoc signo vinces*, "conquer in this sign." In all likelihood, the story was a fabrication, although Constantine *did* have his men paint the *chi-rho*, a cross-like ancient pagan symbol, on their shields—a symbol which, in later years, came to represent Christianity itself.[24]

In some ways, the sudden change was good for the Christian church, because it was once again safe to publicly profess the faith of the Nazarene. But in many respects, Constantine's so-called conversion was also a disaster for Christianity. Whereas previously, only a sincere believer would dare join the Christian church, Christianity suddenly became popular, and the ranks of believers were suddenly flooded with people who wanted to join in order to curry favor with the emperor. There is an old story—possibly apocryphal—in which Constantine even

---

24   Much more detail is given in *Shadow Emperor*.

marched his troops through the river, declaring that they had become Christian because they had all been baptized.

Christianity was in vogue. But it wasn't necessarily growing, because there was now an uncomfortable mix of "believers" in the church. There were those who were sincere followers of Christ, and those who signed on for the perceived benefits and were Christian in name only. March a thousand pagans through a river against their will, after all, and all you get on the other side is an army of wet pagans.

The period of the black horse was a time of famine. A denarius was the typical amount paid for a day's labor; the measures of food for sale at that price were barely a day's worth for a single individual. Anything less would mean starvation. From what we can discern about this ancient grain market, the price being offered was at least 10 times the usual rate.

What does food represent? In the synagogue of Capernaum, Jesus declared Himself to be "the bread which came down from heaven" (John 6:41), and then explained Himself:

> "I am the bread of life. Your fathers ate the manna in the wilderness, and are dead. This is the bread which comes down from heaven, that one may eat of it and not die. I am the living bread which came down from heaven. If anyone eats of this bread, he will live forever; and the bread that I shall give is My flesh, which I shall give for the life of the world."
>
> The Jews therefore quarreled among themselves, saying, "How can this Man give us His flesh to eat?"

Then Jesus said to them, "Most assuredly, I say to you, unless you eat the flesh of the Son of Man and drink His blood, you have no life in you. Whoever eats My flesh and drinks My blood has eternal life, and I will raise him up at the last day. For My flesh is food indeed, and My blood is drink indeed. He who eats My flesh and drinks My blood abides in Me, and I in him. As the living Father sent Me, and I live because of the Father, so he who feeds on Me will live because of Me. This is the bread which came down from heaven—not as your fathers ate the manna, and are dead. He who eats this bread will live forever." (John 6:48-58)

After Constantine, the faith of Jesus was, in the official church of the empire, reduced to mere religion. For most adherents, it was no longer a life-giving connection with the Son of God, but an organization that shadowed the political structure of the empire. Most of the crowd that swelled the church's numbers had little actual interest in the person of Jesus, and openly clung to most of their pagan traditions and rituals, importing them into the church.

The authentic faith of Christ? It became harder and harder to find; the church was plunged into spiritual famine.

In time, those who were insistent on a humble biblical Christianity were pushed to the margins of Constantine's church—setting the stage for the most shameful chapter of Christian history: the Dark Ages. In reality, Rome did not stop persecuting; it merely stopped persecuting those who declared themselves to be Christian. But if a person stepped outside the prescribed bounds of the official church, they would still feel the wrath of the dragon. And now, no longer being persecuted by the pagan Roman Empire of the west, Christians began to persecute each other.

Our history books are shamefully replete with the stories of a Christianity that went off the rails. Professing Christians operated torture chambers and burned people at the stake. Those who dissented from the official church line were labeled heretics and hunted down like wild animals.

The Old Testament was an internal document that highlighted the sins of God's people more than the sins of their neighbors; the same is true of the New Testament: it anticipated the sins of the church.

4. The Pale Horse

> *So I looked, and behold, a pale horse. And the name of him who sat on it was Death, and Hades followed with him. And power was given to them over a fourth of the earth, to kill with sword, with hunger, with death, and by the beasts of the earth.* (Revelation 6:8)

We have already set the table for understanding what happened under the epoch of the pale horse and its rider. By AD 385, the new ecclesiastical version of Rome had formally sentenced its first victim to death for the "crime" of heresy: Priscillian and six of his disciples, who were members of the Manichaean sect.[25]

---

25 The Manichaeans were a sect that blended esoteric gnostic teachings with Christianity in North Africa. Because they were perceived to be a threat to Rome's political stability, they were persecuted by Diocletian, who was accompanied by the young Constantine. After the Christianization of Rome, it was the church itself that persecuted them. *Shadow Emperor* devotes a little space to their story.

The church now took on a pale color—a sickly pale-green—because the church was no longer merely compromising with the emperor . . . it had become sick. Her original mission and message had faded from memory, and she had become more concerned with political pursuits than spiritual ones.

The locus of power for what was left of the empire had pulled to the east, where it survived for a number of centuries with Constantinople as its capital. In the year AD 533, the Emperor Justinian declared the Bishop of Rome the "head of all the holy churches," making him the de facto political power in the west. Bishops and priests had already started filling the political vacuum left behind as Roman forces began to desert their posts. The Romans had divided administrative responsibility across regional units known a *diocese,* and to this day, the older, more formal versions of Christianity continue to use this term to describe administrative regions of the church.

Since the church had already begun filling a political role in the west, Justinian's decree was a natural move. There was a significant challenge, however: the presence of barbarian tribes who, in defiance of the council of Nicaea, continued to hold Arian views, in which the divinity of Christ was held to be something less than equal with the Father. Three groups in particular were troublesome: the Vandals, the Heruli, and the Ostrogoths (eastern Goths).

Thanks to the support of the emperor, by AD 538, all three people groups had been successfully wiped from the map. Most Europeans today can trace their ancestry to some barbarian group—the English to the Angles and Saxons, the French to the Franks, and so on. But the elimination of these three barbarian groups was so complete that we know of no descendants from

the Vandals, Heruli, or Ostrogoths. The Ostrogoths, the last of
the three, laid siege to Rome in AD 537. By the following year,
they had been so thoroughly humiliated by the Roman general
Belisarius that the few remaining survivors disappeared into the
woodwork and were never heard from again.

In the minds of many students of history, then, AD 538
marks the beginning of the period of the pale horse, a time when
ecclesiastical and political powers were so thoroughly blended
in the official version of Christianity that the church became a
mere shadow of the spiritual powerhouse it had been in the first
few centuries. Evangelistic fervor gave way to political conquest.
The Word of God was kept in reserve for the educated class, and
even the liturgy was conducted in a language that few Europeans could understand, let alone read.

It is this period of history that modern Christians continue to find themselves having to explain to skeptics. The cruelty
of ecclesiastical power was on full display, with millions put to
death over the centuries for matters of conscience. People who
disagreed with the official party line had their property confiscated, were sadistically tortured, and were even burned at the stake.

We would do well to pay attention to the fact that it was
predicted in Scripture. Often, modern Christians use some of
the more horrific portions of Bible prophecy as a way to identify moral problems outside of the church, and to be sure, there
are warnings in Scripture to keep ourselves "unspotted from the
world." (James 1:27) But we should not fail to notice that most
of the Old Testament is devoted to identifying the sins of God's
own people. Why should the New Testament be any different?
In fact, most of Paul's letters were written to counteract *internal*
problems, not external ones.

There is a curious passage in Paul's second letter to the
Thessalonians, one that we have already alluded to, that bears
careful examination:

> Now, brethren, concerning the coming of our Lord Jesus
> Christ and our gathering together to Him, we ask you,
> not to be soon shaken in mind or troubled, either by
> spirit or by word or by letter, as if from us, as though the
> day of Christ had come. (2 Thessalonians 2:1, 2)

Paul's first letter to the believers in Thessalonica included
the powerful description of Christ's return found in the 4th
chapter. It apparently so captivated their imaginations that they
came under the impression that the return of Christ was immi-
nent. In his second letter, Paul attempted to put their minds at
ease, pointing out that Jesus will not return until a number of
key events take place:

> Let no one deceive you by any means; for that Day will
> not come unless the falling away comes first, and the
> man of sin is revealed, the son of perdition, who opposes
> and exalts himself above all that is called God or that is
> worshiped, so that he sits as God in the temple of God,
> showing himself that he is God. (2 Thessalonians 2:3, 4)

Christians rightly associate this passage with the Antichrist, but it should be noted that Paul identifies the appearance of the "man of sin" and "son of perdition" as a product of
a "falling away." That is not the language of an external problem; it is the language of apostasy. Something horrible would

happen to Christianity that would pave the way for the man of sin to appear.

> *Do you not remember that when I was still with you I told you these things? And now you know what is restraining, that he may be revealed in his own time. For the mystery of lawlessness is already at work; only He who now restrains will do so until He is taken out of the way.* (2 Thessalonians 2:5-7)

As we have already seen, early Christians identified the power that was restraining the appearance of Antichrist as the Roman Empire. Under Roman persecution, the church had little choice but to remain faithful; half-hearted Christians didn't stick around, waiting to be butchered. But once the pressure had been lifted after the Edict of Milan in AD 313, and the church rolls began to swell with insincere pagans seeking the favor of the empire, the "falling away" could commence, eventually paving the way for the world's biggest problem, the "son of perdition."

Even in Paul's time, he was able to identify a "lawless" power that was taking hold in the church—influences that threatened to corrupt the gospel message. Those harmful influences could not truly break free and blossom into full apostasy until the restraining power of Rome was removed, and then we would enter a phase of religious history in which lawlessness—a disregard for God's moral law—would gather steam.

It is tempting for modern Christians to explain away the darkest chapters of our Christian history—defending what happened, or writing it off as mere ignorance. If we were to be honest with history and the Scriptures, we should probably finally admit that our Christian ancestors strayed from the teachings of Christ . . . and the Bible predicted it would happen.

Jesus never told us to blend church and state; in fact, He specifically stated the opposite:

> *"My kingdom is not of this world. If My kingdom were of this world, My servants would fight, so that I should not be delivered to the Jews; but now My kingdom is not from here."* (John 18:36)

Perhaps it's high time to own what happened, apologize for it, and get back to the business of walking in the footsteps of Jesus and displaying His magnificent character to the world.

There are so many clear warnings in the Bible that we should have seen it coming.

CHAPTER FIVE:
NATIONS FROM THE SEA

THE "MAN OF SIN" OR THE "SON OF PERDITION"
in Paul's prophetic prediction has captivated the imagination of
the church since the letter was first written. Who or what should
we be expecting?

If Paul's description is worrisome, John's description of the
same problem is downright chilling:

> *Then I stood on the sand of the sea. And I saw a beast
> rising up out of the sea, having seven heads and ten
> horns, and on his horns ten crowns, and on his heads
> a blasphemous name. Now the beast which I saw was
> like a leopard, his feet were like the feet of a bear, and his
> mouth like the mouth of a lion. The dragon gave him his
> power, his throne, and great authority. And I saw one of
> his heads as if it had been mortally wounded, and his
> deadly wound was healed. And all the world marveled
> and followed the beast.* (Revelation 13:1-3)

The language, of course, is symbolic; there is no such conglomerate animal in any manual of taxonomy. In the modern
era, people have expended a lot of energy trying to identify

what the symbol means, and it almost seems as if we have had to change our mind every few years. The "beast" has been identified, at various times, as a supercomputer in Belgium, a dictator who seizes power in the European union, and even American presidents ranging from Ronald Reagan to Barack Obama.[26]

Given the pervasive nature of the warning—it appears in many passages of the Bible—it is doubtful that God meant for us to be uncertain, and yet if you wander into a religious bookstore and pick out a dozen books on Bible prophecy, you are likely to get a dozen different theories. Our ancestors in the faith faced no such confusion, however. While many of the details were unclear to some generations because they had not yet been fulfilled, there was widespread agreement on the nature of the beast power. Today, as we find ourselves living in the toes of Nebuchadnezzar's statue, we have many reasons to believe that they knew what they were talking about; even the unclear minor details have been made astonishingly clear.

One of the key reasons we have such broad diversity of opinion on the book of Revelation is that we have largely forgotten how to read it. We approach it as a stand-alone book—something tacked on to the end of the Bible as an ominous harbinger of things to come. When John penned the original manuscript however, he

---

26 The attempt to label Reagan as the Antichrist was not terribly creative—his name, Ronald Wilson Reagan—had three names of six letters, which some insisted gave us 666. The Obama attempt was a little more inventive. Jesus said, in Luke 10:18, "I saw Satan fall like lightning from heaven." The book of Luke was written in Greek, but advocates of the theory suggest that the Hebrew word for lightning is *baraq*. In Isaiah 14:14, Lucifer aspired to ascend "above the heights," which is *bama* in Hebrew. Put it all together—nonsensically, of course—and they insist that Jesus actually said, "I saw Satan fall like Barack Obama."

was building on centuries of biblical interpretation. Something like two-thirds of the imagery and symbols used in Revelation are lifted directly out of other portions of the Bible, a fact that his 1st-century audience would have recognized immediately.

In other words, to read the book of Revelation intelligently, you have to read the whole Bible. There are no shortcuts; John was speaking to a biblically-literate audience.

By far, the most heavily-borrowed material comes from the book of Daniel. There are many allusions to other parts of the Bible, such as Exodus, Jeremiah, and Ezekiel, but Daniel seems to hold a special place as a companion to the book of Revelation. Consider the description of the beast in light of a vision Daniel had many years after Nebuchadnezzar's dream:

> Daniel spoke, saying, "I saw in my vision by night, and behold, the four winds of heaven were stirring up the Great Sea. And four great beasts came up from the sea, each different from the other. The first was like a lion, and had eagle's wings. I watched till its wings were plucked off; and it was lifted up from the earth and made to stand on two feet like a man, and a man's heart was given to it. And suddenly another beast, a second, like a bear. It was raised up on one side, and had three ribs in its mouth between its teeth. And they said thus to it: 'Arise, devour much flesh!' After this I looked, and there was another, like a leopard, which had on its back four wings of a bird. The beast also had four heads, and dominion was given to it. After this I saw in the night visions, and behold, a fourth beast, dreadful and terrible, exceedingly strong. It had huge iron teeth;

it was devouring, breaking in pieces, and trampling the
residue with its feet. It was different from all the beasts
that were before it, and it had ten horns." (Daniel 7:2-7)

The two visions are virtually identical, or at least share the
same elements. Daniel sees four beasts coming out of the sea in
succession; John sees the same four beasts as a strange conglomerate animal rising out of the water. If you count all the heads and
horns in Daniel's dream, you get seven heads (the leopard has four)
and 10 horns, which is the precise number found on John's beast.

Both prophets are describing the same thing, which should
immediately arrest our attention: the warning has been in place
for many centuries. So what does it mean?

When you compare the two chapters side-by-side, the picture that emerges is stunning—and easy to interpret. The ancient Hebrews, once they settled in the land of Canaan, considered themselves to be an island in a sea of Gentiles. (You will
notice that all four animals—the lion, bear, leopard, and fearsome beast—would have been considered ritually unclean, and
unfit for use in the temple services.)

In other prophetic passages, water is said to represent "peo-
ples, multitudes, nations, and tongues." [27] (Revelation 17:15)
When Daniel sees "beasts" rising up from the wind-swept sea,
he is witnessing a succession of Gentile empires rising out of the
winds of strife, or global tumult. How do we know the animals
represent kingdoms? Daniel makes it obvious:

---

27 This explanation proves to be especially pertinent to the subject at hand,
    since the passage in Revelation 17 is describing a great "harlot," a symbol
    used repeatedly throughout the Bible—especially in the prophecies of
    Ezekiel and Jeremiah—referring to believers who have fallen into apostasy.

"Those great beasts, which are four, are four kings which arise out of the earth." (Daniel 7:17)

"The fourth beast shall be a fourth kingdom on earth." (Daniel 7:23)

1. The Winged Lion

The succession of empires presented in Daniel chapter 7 parallels the one we have already studied from Nebuchadnezzar's dream in Daniel chapter 2. Bible prophecy often covers the same ground many times from a number of different angles, reviewing and then expanding the reader's understanding. The first of these animals to rise from the water is a winged lion, a well-known symbol of the Babylonian Empire:

"The first was like a lion, and had eagle's wings. I watched till its wings were plucked off; and it was lifted up from the earth and made to stand on two feet like a man, and a man's heart was given to it." (Daniel 7:4)

The palace of Nebuchadnezzar featured many such winged lions, such as this one photographed by the author some years ago:

Why would the lion have wings? In Scripture, wings (and/or eagles) are often used to represent speed, as with these descriptions of the swiftness of the Chaldean army:

> *"The lion has come up from his thicket, and the destroyer of nations is on his way. He has gone forth from his place to make your land desolate. Your cities will be laid waste, without inhabitant. . . . Behold, he shall come up like clouds, and his chariots like a whirlwind. His horses are swifter than eagles. Woe to us, for we are plundered!"* (Jeremiah 4:7, 13)

> *For indeed I am raising up the Chaldeans, a bitter and hasty nation which marches through the breadth of the earth, to possess dwelling places that are not theirs. They are terrible and dreadful; their judgment and their dignity proceed from themselves. Their horses also are swifter than leopards, and more fierce than evening wolves. Their chargers charge ahead; their cavalry comes from afar; they fly as the eagle that hastens to eat.* (Habakkuk 1:6-8)

The lion represents the same empire that the head of gold represented in Nebuchadnezzar's dream: the Babylonians, whose peak power lasted—approximately—from 605-539 BC.

2. The Ravenous Bear

> *"And suddenly another beast, a second, like a bear. It was raised up on one side, and had three ribs in its mouth between its teeth. And they said thus to it: 'Arise, devour much flesh!'"* (Daniel 7:5)

The power that supplanted the Babylonians, of course, was the coalition empire of the Medes and the Persians, represented in this vision as a lopsided bear, raised up on one side. It is a fitting description—the Medes were the first to rise to power, and were later joined by the Persians, who quickly overshadowed the Medes and became the dominant half of the coalition.

As the Persians swept across Babylonian territory, it conquered three key provinces: Egypt, Lydia, and Babylon—likely represented by the three ribs in the bear's mouth.

The bear represents the same empire that the chest and arms of silver represented in Nebuchadnezzar's dream: the Medes and the Persians, whose peak power lasted approximately from 539-331 BC.

3. The Multi-Winged Leopard

"After this I looked, and there was another, like a leopard, which had on its back four wings of a bird. The beast also had four heads, and dominion was given to it." (Daniel 7:6)

The Greeks, under Alexander the Great, were the next empire to rise out of the struggle for dominion in the ancient world. Alexander, who managed to convince himself that he was descended directly from the gods (he declared himself son of Zeus-Ammon, a hybrid supreme god derived from Greek and Egyptian deities), managed to conquer the known world in record time. He relentlessly pushed his men on a march from Macedonia to India, which many assumed to be the end of the earth.

Upon reaching India, his troops began to grumble intensely; they hadn't been home in years, and even though they had been encouraged to pick up foreign wives along the way, they'd had enough and wanted to go home. Reluctantly, Alexander boarded his men on ships and began the long trek back to Babylon. From there, he actually intended to push southward into Arabia instead of returning home, but died before it could happen.

The cause of Alexander's death remains something of a mystery. He had been severely wounded a number of times on the battlefield, and had also succumbed to a serious bout of disease (possibly typhoid or West Nile Virus). Even then, he could have possibly survived except for one additional factor: his passion for excessive drinking. Those who were present in Babylon recorded that in one evening, Alexander drank in an inordinate amount of wine, and was dead shortly thereafter.

He was 32 years old when he died. He had managed to conquer the known world with unbelievable speed, but it is possible he never managed to conquer his own passions. The lion had eagle's wings, denoting rapid conquest; the leopard has a double set of wings, which is entirely fitting: Alexander seized an impressive amount of territory—more than 2 million square miles—in just four short years.

After his death, there was a brief power struggle, and the empire was divided among four of his generals: Lysimachus, Ptolemy, Cassander, and Seleucus. Amazingly, before Alexander had drawn his first breath as an infant, Daniel saw this detail in the four heads of the leopard. The Macedonians reigned supreme from about 331 until 168 BC.

Based on Nebuchadnezzar's dream, you probably know which empire is next. If you guessed Rome, you're exactly right.

4. The Fearsome Beast

"After this I saw in the night visions, and behold, a fourth beast, dreadful and terrible, exceedingly strong. It had huge iron teeth; it was devouring, breaking in pieces, and trampling the residue with its feet. It was different from all the beasts that were before it, and it had ten horns." (Daniel 7:7)

The beast with iron teeth corresponds to the iron legs of Nebuchadnezzar's statue. The Romans were the empire still ruling the world when Christ was born, and Jesus died on a Roman cross. After winning the battle of Pydna in 168 BC, Macedonian supremacy was finally broken and Rome's primacy was unquestionable. As we have already seen, Rome's might in the west would continue for more than 500 years, until the last Western emperor was finally deposed in AD 476.

As with the statue of Daniel 2, the division of the Roman Empire is also present in this prophecy. Beasts are used to represent kings and kingdoms, and horns are often used to represent the same thing. There are 10 horns growing from the fearsome beast's head, just as there were 10 toes on the statue. After the Western Roman Empire collapsed, its territory fragmented into barbarian kingdoms, which eventually became the nations of Western Europe that we know today:

"The ten horns are ten kings who shall arise from this kingdom." (Daniel 7:24)

Up to this point, the prophecy of Daniel chapter 7 has all been review, covering the same historical time periods as the prophecy of Daniel chapter 2. But even though there are no more beasts that rise out of the sea, there is more to the story, and now it is time to move into slow gear and examine the text carefully. A fifth power rises out of the Roman Empire, and it is at this point that the merger of church and state inaugurated by Constantine suddenly shows up in the book of Daniel.

5. The Little Horn

> "I was considering the horns, and there was another horn, a little one, coming up among them, before whom three of the first horns were plucked out by the roots. And there, in this horn, were eyes like the eyes of a man, and a mouth speaking pompous words." (Daniel 7:8)

As Daniel is contemplating the 10 kings who emerge from the shattered Roman Empire, he suddenly notices another, smaller horn emerging among them. For centuries, students of Bible prophecy have recognized that this little horn is something of an Antichrist figure, and bad news for God's people. What some students miss, however, is the correlation between this little horn and the conglomerate beast from the sea that John sees in the 13th chapter of Revelation. When you compare the descriptions, there is little doubt: both John and Daniel are describing the same thing.

And when you start to jot down the biblical descriptors of this mysterious power, it doesn't take long for a very clear picture to emerge. For long centuries, virtually all Christian scholars understood, very clearly, who or what the little horn represented. It is only in modern times that we have become confused—constantly changing our minds about its identity.

Let's examine the evidence carefully:

1. It is a *little* **horn** that comes up among the others. If it comes up among the others, it must appear in Western Europe, but it is smaller than other European kingdoms.

2. It must appear **after AD 476**, because that is the date after which the 10 horns appear, and this little horn emerges from among them.

3. The little horn **destroys three of the other kingdoms**, "before whom three of the first horns were plucked out by the roots." (Daniel 7:8) Daniel 7:24 repeats this, telling us that the little horn "shall subdue three kings."

4. Daniel 7:24 also tells us that this kingdom will be "**different from the first ones.**" There is something unusual about the nature of this kingdom.

5. Daniel 7:25 tells us that the little horn power will "**speak pompous words against the Most High.**" Revelation 13:5 tells us that this power speaks "great things and blasphemies."

It is useful at this point to determine what is meant by "great things and blasphemies." Today, many people consider using God's name as an expletive to be blasphemy, but the biblical understanding of blasphemy runs much deeper. This power is not merely using God's name inappropriately; it is claiming to have the attributes of God Himself. Notice how the religious leaders of Jesus' day accused Him of blasphemy:

The Jews answered Him, saying, "For a good work we do not stone You, but for blasphemy, and because You, being a Man, make Yourself God." (John 10:33)

Jesus, of course, was *not* committing blasphemy, since He *was* God in human flesh. But when the religious authorities of the day perceived that He was claiming divinity, they didn't believe it and accused Him of usurping the place of God—the biblical definition of blaspheming.

There is another example, in which Jesus was accused of blasphemy for claiming an attribute that belongs to God alone, the ability to forgive sins:

"Why does this Man speak blasphemies like this? Who can forgive sins but God alone?" (Mark 2:7)

The little horn power claims to hold the place of God, which is precisely what Paul predicted about the "man of sin" in his second letter to the Thessalonians:

Let no one deceive you by any means; for that Day will not come unless the falling away comes first, and the man of sin is revealed, the son of perdition, who opposes and exalts himself above all that is called God or that is worshiped, so that he sits as God in the temple of God, showing himself that he is God. (2 Thessalonians 2:3, 4)[28]

---

28 It is useful to notice Paul's assertion that this "man of sin" or "son of perdition" would appear on earth before Jesus comes for the church. Many expositors of Bible prophecy now say that this Antichrist figure appears *after* the rapture of the church, but what Paul writes suggests otherwise.

There are a few more important descriptors we should notice:

6. The little horn power is **a persecuting power**. Daniel 7:25 tells us that it will "persecute the saints of the Most High," and Revelation 13:7 predicts that it would be "granted unto him to make war with the saints and overcome them."

7. It would **reign for a specific period of time,** after which its power would wane. Daniel 7:25 identifies this period of time as "a time and times and half a time." Revelation 13:5 suggests it would be "given authority for forty-two months."

These two periods of time—a "time and times and half a time," and 42 months—are identical. A "time" is simply a year, as indicated by the story in Daniel 4, where Nebuchadnezzar loses his sanity for a period of seven "times," or years. "Times" is simply two years; "half a time" is half a year. This is describing a period of three-and-a-half years, or 42 months.

It also happens to be 1,260 days. (The Hebrew year had 360 days; any time the calendar seemed to be a little off, an extra month was inserted to bring it back into alignment.) The woman, who represents the church that Satan persecutes in Revelation 12, has to go into hiding in the wilderness for this same period of time: 1,260 days, or 42 months, or three-and-a-half years.

These are not literal days, however. In the language of prophecy, *days* are symbolic, representing *years*:

> *"For I have laid on you the years of their iniquity, according to the number of the days, three hundred and ninety days; so you shall bear the iniquity of the house of Israel. And when you have completed them, lie again on your right side; then you shall bear the iniquity of the*

*house of Judah forty days. I have laid on you a day for
each year."* (Ezekiel 4:5, 6)

*"According to the number of the days in which you spied
out the land, forty days, for each day you shall bear your
guilt one year, [namely] forty years, and you shall know
My rejection."* (Numbers 14:34)

The 1,260 days—or 42 months—then represents a significant period of time: 1,260 literal years.

We have now easily gathered enough evidence[29] to determine who or what the little horn—and the beast of Revelation 13—represent. Line up the descriptors side by side, and a chilling picture emerges:

- It is a small kingdom that emerges among the barbarians of the west.
- It emerges after AD 476.
- It uproots three of the barbarian tribes.
- It is a different kind of kingdom, distinct from the others.
- It speaks "great words" or blasphemy.
- It is a persecuting power.
- It wields power for 1,260 prophetic days, or literal years.

For the last century and a half, Christians have unfortunately been looking in all the wrong places for this emerging power. We have searched for a dictator in Europe, a supercomputer in Belgium, and in a thousand other places. But we have forgotten

---

29 There is more, but we have enough for the moment.

that the warnings of the Bible are leveled at God's own people far more often than at others. The Old Testament identifies the sins of Israel, and the New Testament predicts the sins of the church.

There is no question who or what the little horn represents: it is *us*. It is the dominant organized Christian church after Constantine. For long centuries, right up to the modern age, Christian scholars have recognized this, and have warned God's people that something was amiss *inside* Christianity, because the description tragically fits official Christianity like a glove:

1. **It is a small kingdom that emerges among the barbarians of the west**. Ask yourself: did Christianity in the Middle Ages create a small kingdom or power in the remnants of the Western Empire? The answer is *yes*: and it still persists to this day, as one of the smallest nation-states in the world, the very embodiment of the marriage of church and state: the Vatican State.

2. **It must emerge as a distinct power after AD 476**. This is certainly the case. Remember: as the political Roman Empire retreated into the east, it was in AD 533 that the Emperor Justinian handed power over the west to the Bishop of Rome.

3. **It destroys three of the barbarian kingdoms**. This is also true. There were, as we have already seen, three barbarian tribes that refused to acknowledge the supremacy of the Bishop of Rome: the Vandals, the Heruli, and the Ostrogoths. The last of these, the Ostrogoths, were demolished in AD 538; none of these barbarian tribes exist today. Exactly as predicted, Roman troops came to the aid of the Bishop of Rome and eliminated three of the horns. Remember the year AD 538, when the power promised to the Bishop of Rome by Justinian became a reality; it will prove important in a moment.

4. **It would be a different sort of kingdom**. Who could argue this one? As the Western Roman Empire crumbled, clergy filled the administrative roles in the west. The official church of the Dark Ages was not ruled by monarchs or run by parliamentarians; it was a blend of church and state, brought on by Constantine's so-called conversion. The supreme ruler was the Pontiff, the one who claimed to represent God on earth.

5. **It would speak "great words" or "blasphemy."** This may be the most embarrassing part of our Christian history. As the Western world plunged into the darkness of the Middle Ages, Christian clergy began to make some rather ostentatious claims for themselves. In the 9th century, Pope Nicholas I said the unthinkable:

> *"I am all in all, and above all, so that God Himself, and I, the Vicar of God, hath both one consistory, and I am able to do almost all that God can do."*[30]

Pope Pius V said something disturbingly similar:

> *"The Pope and God are the same, so he has all power in Heaven and earth."*[31]

Ferraris' Ecclesiastical Dictionary, assembled in the 18th century, underscored the claim:

> *"The Pope is of so great dignity and so exalted that he is not a mere man, but as it were God .... The Pope is*

---

30   Pope Nicholas I, *Decret. Par. Distinct 96*, Chapter 7.

31   Cited in William Barclay, *Cities Petrus Bertanous*. 218.

called most holy because he is rightfully presumed to be
such . . . . hence the Pope is crowned with a triple crown,
as king of heaven, and of earth, and of the lower region.
Moreover, the superiority and the power of the Roman
Pontiff by no means pertain only to heavenly things, to
earthly things, and to things under the earth, but are
even over angels, than whom he is greater. So that if it
were possible that the angels might err from the faith,
they could be judged and excommunicated by the Pope.
For he is of so great dignity and power that he forms one
and the same tribunal with Christ. So that whatever the
Pope does, seems to proceed from the mouth of God. The
Pope is, as it were, God on earth."[32]

Our Christian history throughout the Dark Ages is replete
with pompous claims that are reminiscent of the arrogance
of Roman caesars. As we assumed the reins of power in the
crumbling Western Empire, we tragically also assumed their
attitudes, which is why many historians refer to the Medieval
church as a period of "Caesaropapism," the Bishop of Rome
having taken the place of the emperor. And as the caesars
claimed divinity for themselves, so did we.

It is one of our darkest chapters as a church, but we must admit, it fits.

6. **It would be a persecuting power**. We scarcely need to cite
   specific examples to know that Medieval Christianity was
   guilty of persecuting those who disagreed with formally-rec-

---

32 *Ferraris' Ecclesiastical Dictionary*, Vol. 6.

ognized doctrine. For long centuries, untold millions were put to death over matters of conscience. Heretics were tortured in an attempt to change their minds, and many were put to death. The Spanish Inquisition, for example, sentenced more than 1,400 people from various cities around Spain to be burned at the stake in the first half of the 17th century alone.[33] Some historical estimates have placed the death toll for the whole period of the Dark Ages (ranging from about the 6th century to the 19th) in excess of 50 million people.

It was not only dissenting Christians who met with persecution, however. Shortly after the Christianization of the Roman Empire, Emperor Theodosius turned the tables on pagans, declaring their religious practices to be illegal and threatening the death penalty if they continued in them:

> *"No one shall consult a soothsayer, astrologer or diviner. The perverse pronouncements of augurs and seers must fall silent. . . . The universal curiosity about divination must be silent forever. Whosoever refuses obedience to this command shall suffer the penalty of death and be laid low by the avenging sword." —Codex Theodosianus, IX.16.4*[34]

Armed with the political machinery of the empire, Christians started doing to others what Rome had done to them from the late 4th century forward. It is to our shame that we have

---

33 Teofanes Egido, *Las Modificaciones de la Tipologia: Nueva Estructura Delictiva*, in: Joaquín Pérez Villanueva & Bartolomé Escandell Bonet, *Historia de la Inquisición en España y América*, Vol. 1. Madrid 1984, 1395.

34 Croke, Brian and Jill Harries (eds). *Religious Conflict in Fourth-Century Rome: A Documentary Study.* Sydney: Macarthur Press, 1982, n.p.

so often failed to follow the teachings and example of Christ. Modern skeptics love to highlight this period of history in an attempt to discredit the Christian faith, suggesting that the Bible must be flawed. The student of Bible prophecy, however, quickly recognizes that the Bible not only never condones this kind of behavior for the church, but it also warned us it was coming.

7. It would **reign for 1,260 days;** each day standing for a year. The Emperor Justinian, ruling from Constantinople in the east, suddenly elevated the power and position of the Bishop of Rome in the west with his decree of AD 533. As we have already seen, there were three barbarian groups who were not compliant: the Vandals, the Heruli, and the Ostrogoths. The last of these was defeated in AD 538, making the Bishop of Rome's new-found power a reality.

The elevated status of the Bishop of Rome persisted more or less unchecked until the late 18th century, when it was suddenly arrested by Napoleon's troops. In December of 1797, Joseph Bonaparte, Napoleon's older brother and ambassador to Rome, threw a "republican" party at his palace—a party meant to encourage the overthrow of monarchy and the establishment of a republican government, as had happened in France. The party spilled into the streets and swelled into a riot. When Pope Pius VI heard of the unrest, he sent in troops to quell it, and in the process, killed Mathurin-Léonard Duphot, one of Napoleon's generals.

For months, Pius VI had been trying to dissuade Napoleon from making any further advancement toward Rome. The death of the general, however, was enough to convince Napoleon to act. On February 10, 1798, General Louis-Alexandre

Berthier marched into the Eternal City, declared a republic, and demanded that Pius VI renounce his temporal authority. The Pope naturally refused, and on February 20, he was taken prisoner and escorted out of the city. He died a prisoner.

It was 1798: precisely 1,260 years after the Bishop of Rome's temporal authority had become a reality in AD 538.

The picture that emerges from Bible prophecy is stunning. The details we have examined so far scarcely skim the surface of the biblical data; the more you study chapters like Daniel 7, Daniel 8, 2 Thessalonians 2, Revelation 13, and Revelation 17, the more obvious it becomes that the little horn power—the sea beast of Revelation 13—is not some mysterious and unwelcome outsider who pushes his way into the church, or a mere politician who seizes global power in the last few years of earth's history. The warnings of Scripture are leveled at God's own people, because the problem is *us*. Just as God's people in the Old Testament wandered away from their original calling, so did we. It is hard to deny it; our history books are glutted with sobering examples of our own apostasy from the faith of Jesus.

For many, the realization that Christianity's biggest problems are internal explains a deep-seated feeling that something is wrong with organized religion. There is. While Christians are certainly also responsible for much good in the world, the way Christianity has been shaped over the last 2,000 years has meant a noticeable disconnect from the church portrayed in the New Testament.

What happened to *that* church? Did it simply disappear as state-sponsored religion took the faith of Jesus in a dark new direction? Or did the teachings of Jesus manage to persist in spite of the dark shadow that began to spread across the former Roman Empire? The powerful white horse that conquered the Roman Empire with the good news of the gospel was tragically transformed into a sickly pale horse. What became of authentic, biblical Christianity?

The answer is breathtaking.

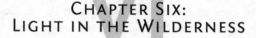

CHAPTER SIX:
LIGHT IN THE WILDERNESS

Now when the dragon saw that he had been cast to the earth, he persecuted the woman who gave birth to the male Child. But the woman was given two wings of a great eagle, that she might fly into the wilderness to her place, where she is nourished for a time and times and half a time, from the presence of the serpent. (Revelation 12:13, 14)

TWENTY YEARS AFTER ALARIC RODE INTO THE city of Rome, the church father Augustine of Hippo was dying. On his deathbed, he could hear yet another wave of barbarians attacking his own city in North Africa. It was becoming clearer by the day that Rome was finished; everywhere, jubilant barbarians were seizing imperial territory with relative impunity.

Roman pagans decried the successful invasions as evidence that the pagan gods were angry about Constantine's Christianization of the empire. Augustine had just finished his literary masterpiece, *The City of God*, in which he argued that the fall of the empire had nothing to do with Christianity. The barbarians, he pointed out, had great respect for Christianity and even spared those who sought refuge in Christian churches:

> *The reliquaries of the martyrs and the churches of the apostles bear witness to this; for in the sack of the city they were open sanctuary for all who fled to them, whether Christian or Pagan. To their very threshold the blood-thirsty enemy raged; there his murderous fury owned a limit. Thither did such of the enemy as had any pity convey those to whom they had given quarter, lest any less mercifully disposed might fall upon them. And, indeed, when even those murderers who everywhere else showed themselves pitiless came to those spots where that was forbidden which the license of war permitted in every other place, their furious rage for slaughter was bridled, and their eagerness to take prisoners was quenched. Thus escaped multitudes who now reproach the Christian religion, and impute to Christ the ills that have befallen their city; but the preservation of their own life—a boon which they owe to the respect entertained for Christ by the barbarians—they attribute not to our Christ, but to their own good luck.*[35]

Augustine's book would be one of the final works to emerge from the pen of classical antiquity; after the fall of Rome, the age of pagan culture and learning came to an abrupt end because (largely) illiterate barbarians had little use for Greek and Roman intellectual achievement.

---

35   Augustine of Hippo. *The City of God*. Waxkeep Publishing. Print, Kindle, 2.

It is understandable that the barbarian invaders had little respect for the so-called civilized countries. The Romans, and the Greeks before them, held the barbarians in utter contempt, insisting that they were crude, unlearned, and uncivilized. Even their language was rudimentary, it was argued, and sounded like nonsense. The name *barbarian* itself was—and still is—a pejorative term, and may have originated from the practice of making fun of barbarian tongues: "bar, bar, bar, bar—that's all those people can say!" A barbarian, then, was someone who spoke a simple, uneducated language.

As the Western Empire collapsed, the hallmarks of civilization were being destroyed. As the author Thomas Cahill points out, "A world in chaos is not a world in which books are copied and libraries maintained."[36] The world came within a hair's breadth of losing all of its intellectual attainments: Plato, Aristotle, Socrates, and almost every other masterpiece of classical thought.

Tragically, that also meant that Christianity itself was now in peril.

From the time of Constantine forward, the Christian church had been deeply influenced by Roman politics and government. As previously noted, the church was suddenly flooded with half-hearted Christians who only joined because of the implied prestige and social benefits. The hardy fiber of a group of determined believers who had held the church together throughout the years of Roman persecution now began to weaken and disintegrate through a process of dilution and politicization.

---

36 Cahill, Thomas. *How the Irish Saved Civilization*. New York: Doubleday, 1995, 35.

Two key controversies that erupted in Christianity after the rise of Constantine helped to establish Rome as a key center of influence in the Christian world: the Donatist Controversy and the Arian Controversy. The Donatist Controversy broke out in North Africa when members of the clergy who had fled the church during persecution suddenly wanted back in. Those who had stayed the course referred to them as *traditores*—traitors—and refused re-admittance. Some insisted that the sins of the traitors were so grave that even any baptisms performed by them in the past were invalid.

The Donatists pushed hard to have their leader, Donatus Magnus, installed as the Bishop of Carthage in place of Caecilian, the current bishop who favored returning the errant clergy to church membership. The controversy grew so heated that it threatened to rip the church in half, something that concerned Constantine greatly. Aware of the church's perseverance under pagan Roman persecution, he had been counting on the Christians to help unite his new consolidated empire.

Unable to solve the issue themselves, the church in North Africa had turned to Constantine for help. Constantine wrote:

> *"So great a madness persists in [the Donatists] that with incredible arrogance they repudiate the equitable judgment that has been given, so that, by the will of heaven, I have learnt that they demand my own judgment. . . . They demand my judgment when I myself await the judgment of Christ."*[37]

---

37 Stephenson, Paul. *Constantine: Roman Emperor, Christian Victor.* Overlook Press, 2010, 262.

Constantine believed that if he could not bring unity to the Christian church, God would stop favoring him, and he would never be able unite the Roman Empire. Angry, he told the African church that if they didn't get their act together, he was going to come down in person and show them how to run a church. If anyone objected, then, well, to quote Constantine himself: "These without doubt I shall cause to suffer the due penalties of their madness and their reckless obstinacy."[38]

The Donatist Controversy provided some of the earliest indications that the church was about to start persecuting non-compliant believers. We have some indication that those who refused to comply with Constantine's wishes for peace faced the death penalty; according to some sources, Caecilian eventually rounded up his opponents with the help of the Roman authorities and had them put to death.[39]

Perhaps the most important development to emerge from the Donatist Controversy was the appeal to the head of state for help in solving problems in the church. It was the beginnings of an ill-fated relationship between church and state, in which the Bishop of Rome naturally began to rise in prominence because of his proximity to the Eternal City. The second dispute emerged when a renegade priest by the name of Arius began to teach an alternate understanding of the nature of Christ, one which demoted Him to an inferior position to the Father, and suggested that He was, to some extent, a created Being.

Again, when the church found itself unable to bring the dispute to a close on its own, it appealed to the emperor for

---

38   Ibid., 263.

39   Ibid.

help, which eventually led to the famous Council of Nicaea in the city of Nicaea—İznik in modern-day Turkey. The result was the Nicene Creed, which carefully explained the certainties of Christian doctrine and underscored the full divinity of Christ. More importantly, it was once again assumed that the state had a place in the life of the church.[40]

After Constantine, the influence of the Bishop of Rome began to grow, and the city of Rome gradually became the world's key center of Christian influence. When the Western Empire began to collapse, Christian learning and scholarship suddenly found itself in peril along with the classical learning of the pagans. The secular government of Rome began to pull rapidly to the east, to Constantinople, leaving Roman-style Christian bishops as the last civic authority figures in the crumbling west. An empire once ruled by caesars and senators was now ruled by bishops, who became the new faces of Roman law and order.

To the far north, in places like Britannia, Roman armies started going home because their efforts were no longer sustainable without the backing of Rome. The retreat of Roman forces emboldened Germanic barbarian tribes to move from the mainland into the newly vacant regions. Beginning in the 5th century, the Saxons crossed the water into the British Isles, pushing Celtic Britons into Wales and Cornwall.

There was pressure from the Western frontier, too: Celtic pirates from Ireland began raiding the coast, stealing British children to be sold into slavery. They were some of the most-feared people in the ancient world: rough, violent, and shockingly promiscuous. Those who witnessed them on the battle-

---

40   Both controversies are discussed in more detail in *Shadow Emperor.*

field described them as non-human—demons from pits of hell. Under the cover of night, they would cross the sea in small skin-covered boats, called *coracles,* which they commanded so masterfully that they were able to explore as far abroad as Iceland. In the darkest part of the morning, Celtic raiders would slip silently into British homes and then be halfway back to Ireland with captive children before the parents woke up and realized what had happened.

At about the same time that Alaric was marching into the north of Italy, and just a few years before he sacked the city of Rome, Irish raiders kidnapped a 16-year-old British boy by the name of Pātricius. He was taken back to Ireland and forced to work as a shepherd slave for an Irish king by the name of Miliucc.[41] For six long years, Pātricius—or Patrick, as he is called today—tended sheep in the chilly countryside of a land the Romans called *Hibernia,* the land of winter.

Shepherding is a contemplative life, giving its practitioner a lot of time to think. As Patrick sat in the field with his sheep, he started to think about the Christian God his father worshipped. Before his abduction, he had considered Christianity to be a religion for fools, but as a slave, it began to speak to him, as it had to countless Roman slaves in the earliest days of the church.

Fortunately for us, Patrick thought to record his experience:

> *Tending flocks was my daily work, and I would pray constantly during the daylight hours. The love of God and the fear of him surrounded me more and more— and faith grew and the Spirit was roused, so that in one*

---

41 In reality, Irish "kings" were little more than tribal chieftains who ruled over a handful of families.

day I would say as many as a hundred prayers and after
dark nearly as many again, even while I remained in
the woods or on the mountain. I would wake and pray
before daybreak—through snow, frost, rain—nor was
there any sluggishness in me (such as I experience now-
adays) because then the Spirit within me was ardent.[42]

As has been the case with millions of people, Patrick found
comfort in the religion of Jesus at the lowest point in his life.
This was also the case with Constantine's mother, Helena, who
likely turned to Christianity after her divorce from Constantine's
father, who considered her peasant upbringing a barrier to his
advancement in the empire. Young, alone, and enslaved, Patrick
suddenly found great appeal in Jesus, and readily converted.

His conversion proved to be one of the great turning points
in history. One night, he suddenly heard a voice calling to him
in his dreams: "Patrick, your hungers are rewarded; you are going home."

He woke up, certain that it was nothing but a dream, but
amazingly, the voice continued to speak. "Look, your ship is
ready."

Patrick rose to his feet and walked about 200 miles to
the sea, through a countryside he had likely never seen. Sure
enough, he eventually found a merchant ship that agreed, after some discussion, to take him away from Ireland in spite of
the fact that he was penniless. What happened over the next
few years is not exactly clear, and has likely been embellished by
those seeking to make his life seem even more sensational than

---

42   Cahill, Thomas. *How the Irish Saved Civilization*. New York: Doubleday,
     1995, 102.

it already is. What we do know is that he probably wandered the European mainland, likely Gaul, for an unknown period of time, after which he returned to his family in Britain.

His family, naturally, hoped he would stay home for the rest of his life. But it was not meant to be: Patrick had another dream, this time of a man he had known back in Ireland. In the dream, the man was now identified as Patrick's angel, and he was holding a batch of letters. He pulled one out and handed it to Patrick. At the top, it said *Vox Hiberionacum,* or *The Voice of the Hibernians—The Voice of the Irish.* As Patrick clutched the letter, he suddenly heard the voice of a large crowd pleading with him to come back to Ireland: "We beg you to come and walk among us once more."

At first, he ignored it, but the dreams kept coming, and eventually, Patrick said, he heard the voice of Jesus Himself. *"He who gave his life for you; he it is who speaks within you."*

That was the deciding moment. He returned to Gaul to study for the ministry, and then—amazingly—he traveled to Ireland, to live among the people who had stolen his youth.

He established himself in Ard Mhacha, modern-day Armagh. From there, he began to share the gospel with some of the roughest people on the planet. Amazingly, they listened, and the Irish began to turn to Christianity. Even the legendary High King Aengus was baptized at the Rock of Cashel. Patrick carried a crozier, a stylized shepherd's crook still seen in many churches today, and it had a sharp spike on the bottom that allowed him to plant it in the ground when he wasn't holding it. At the king's baptism, he attempted to jab it into the ground, and inadvertently planted it in the king's foot. The king, surprisingly, didn't utter a word. When he was later asked why he didn't protest the impalement of his foot, he remarked that he had thought it was part of the ceremony—an understandable misconception among a tough-minded people used to feats of strength and endurance.

Ireland was utterly transformed by Patrick's efforts. He managed to establish centers of Christian learning and the influence of Christian thought was widely felt. The slave trade, for example, came to a quick end after the first emancipation campaign in the history of the world. The wars between various Irish chieftains, once a regular feature of Celtic life, suddenly waned to an all-time low among a fiercely passionate people who now embraced the Prince of Peace.

We have few written records of Christian missionaries who traveled to remote areas of the globe between the close of the New Testament and the collapse of Rome, even though there is little doubt they existed; to suggest that they did not ignores the clear passion of 1st-century believers. Patrick is likely the first willing missionary to deliberately choose to bring the gospel to a barbarian tribe outside of the empire. Of course, we do know of Ulfilas, but he was already living among the Goths, the son of captives, when he began to share the Christian faith with his captors. Patrick returned to Ireland of his own volition.

The timing of his return is intriguing. Between the years of AD 410 and 476, the stability Constantine brought to the empire was rapidly evaporating, and the political machinery of the west was on a fast track to oblivion. Clergy who had compromised with Constantine were filling the roles once held by administrators who had departed for the east, and the essential doctrines of New Testament Christianity were becoming lost as the church grew more and more political. At that same moment,

Patrick descended on an island remote from the empire, bringing a more pristine version of the Christian faith to Celtic barbarians who cared nothing for the power structures of Rome.

A Christianity more closely aligned with the message and mission of the 1st-century church suddenly, improbably, emerged at the edge of the world. Coincidence?

It provides a fascinating case study to those who wonder what Christianity *might* have looked like had it not compromised with pagan Roman politics. What kind of church would emerge if the man who had established it had not been part of the great compromise taking place on the European continent?

Early Celtic Christianity was a distinctly non-Roman version of the faith, free from the cultural and political baggage of imperial Rome. It was both markedly Irish in its culture *and* biblical in its belief. Early Celtic missionaries were brilliant proselytizers, doggedly refusing to strip away the culture of their converts. The Irish were allowed to remain Irish, whereas converts to Christianity on the mainland were more or less compelled to conform to the cultural norms of the Roman Empire. Patrick and others observed their audiences carefully—a skill the Apostle Paul also used to his advantage[43]—and used aspects of their own cultural beliefs to introduce biblical concepts.

So, for example, they noticed that the Irish were passionate about the land they lived on, and had established a detailed pagan belief system that tied them to nature in a very intimate way. To them, the land was almost alive. Instead of abolishing the Celtic love of nature in order to rid them of their paganism, early missionaries spent much time talking about the one true Creator

---

43   See Acts 14:9, for example.

God who had gifted the world to the human race. They validated the Irish love for nature, while subtly moving them away from a pantheistic worldview. The stone circles and Neolithic monuments that dotted the countryside were not pulled down; rather, they came to be replaced by the characteristic high crosses that now dot Christian Celtic graveyards.

The Celts were passionate storytellers, and took to literacy with zeal, abandoning pagan idols and human sacrifices for the world of letters. Within the space of a few short years, they learned to read and write the languages of mainland Europe, and passionately collected and copied books in their monasteries. Their sudden appetite for letters proved to be one of the most important developments in world history—because in addition to collecting the works of classical antiquity, they also copied the Bible. As the libraries of established civilization were burning, the remote land of Hibernia became the place where the Christian Scriptures survived as the rest of Europe plunged into the darkness caused by both a crumbling empire and an illicit marriage of church and state.

The transformation of the Celts was remarkable; the pagan Irish had been big, loud, and powerful. They loved oversized gestures and big feasts. But the *Christian* Irish? They were different. They suddenly delighted in simplicity and modesty, preferring a humble lifestyle in close contact with nature. They lived in simple abbeys—centers of learning run by pious Irish monks who lived in modest stone structures, governed not by bishops and archbishops, but by abbots, who also served as chaplains to the powerful families of Ireland.

The Irish monks—usually 13 to an abbey (an abbot with 12 disciples)—spent their days preaching, teaching, learning,

and carefully copying the Scriptures. A large part of the reason
we have Bibles in our possession today is because faithful Celtic scholars made absolutely certain the Bible didn't disappear
in the chaos of the Dark Ages. Their monasteries emerged all
across the land, in some very remarkable remote places, like
Skellig Michael, an island refuge in the North Atlantic, which
is still standing more than 1,500 years after it was built. From
this and other centers of learning, Irish monks began to travel
across Europe, collecting every scrap of literature they could lay
their hands on, carefully making copies and preserving them for
future generations.

The hand-illuminated manuscripts they produced were
stunning—some of the most beautiful manuscripts in the history of Western civilization. The Irish had, and still have, a strong
sense of the artistic. Their writing was beautiful, poetic. To this
day, the shelves of bookstores are still dotted with the names of
great Celtic literary geniuses like James Joyce, Samuel Beckett,
C.S. Lewis, Oscar Wilde, Jonathan Swift, Bram Stoker, William
Yeats—and countless others.

The Celts, who embodied a blend of fierce passion and artistic beauty, were *exactly* the right people to preserve the apostolic Christian faith on the edges of the European wilderness,
safely secluded from the compromise and corruption that was
degrading the mainstream church. Wild and passionate, artistic
and determined, they were the kind of people who would not
only preserve the faith, but do it with style.

Much of the literature of the early Celtic church has been
preserved and handed down to us, and it is a sheer delight to
read, bubbling with vibrant personality. One 9th-century Irish
monk, apparently distracted by his cat while copying a com-

mentary on Virgil, slipped his own poem into the manuscript,
giving us a glimpse into his daily life:

> *I and Pangur Ban, my cat,*
> *'Tis a like task we are at;*
> *Hunting mice is his delight,*
> *Hunting words I sit all night.*
>
> *'Tis a merry thing to see*
> *At our tasks how glad are we,*
> *When at home we sit and find*
> *Entertainment to our mind.*
>
> *'Gainst the wall he sets his eye,*
> *Full and fierce and sharp and sly;*
> *'Gainst the wall of knowledge I*
> *All my little wisdom try.*
>
> *So in peace our task we ply,*
> *Pangur Ban, my cat, and I;*
> *In our arts we find our bliss,*
> *I have mine and he has his.*[44]

The Celts were able scholars, masters of language who
worked well in Greek, Hebrew, and Latin. But in spite of their
high linguistic achievement, they were careful to preserve the
Scriptures in the common language of the people they were
teaching. As mainline Christianity was tragically obscuring

---

44 Cahill, Thomas. *How the Irish Saved Civilization*. New York: Doubleday,
    1995, 162.

the gospel by veiling it in the dead language of a vanished empire, unavailable to the average villager, the Celtic missionaries preached in Gaelic. Why did Rome use Latin? It was the dignified, educated language of the empire, and the Scriptures were considered too sacred to be sullied by the uneducated masses, particularly in barbarian Europe. Those who wanted to know what Jesus taught would have to ask the clergy. But not so with the Celts: they knew the writings of the prophets and apostles belonged to everybody. To their way to thinking, it was more important to disseminate the contents of the Bible than to venerate the book itself.

The beliefs of the early Celtic Christians are important to consider, because they were incubated in a region that was largely free from Roman influence, and they give us a good idea of what European Christianity would have looked like had it not been filtered through the emperor's palace. Fortunately, the Irish love of writing means that they have left us a record of what they believed.

One of the first things that stands out in the life of Patrick is his love for the Bible. We still have two important works that Patrick wrote: his *Confession* and a short letter. Neither of these documents is long, but in the space of a few short pages, Patrick manages to quote the Bible no fewer than 340 times. For the Celts, the Bible was the ultimate arbiter of truth and the rule of faith. Human opinion and the judgments of human church councils were subject to the authority of Scripture. At a time when mainline European Christianity was starting to adopt hundreds—maybe thousands—of manmade customs and pagan Roman traditions, the Celtic Christians were building a new church based primarily on the words of the Bible.

The Venerable Bede, one of England's most notable church historians, marveled at how doggedly the Irish stuck with the Bible. When Roman-style Christianity began to examine the faith of the Celts, they entered into a dispute about the date on which Easter should be celebrated. Speaking of the Celtic missionary and luminary, Aidan, he admiringly observed:

> To be brief, so far as I have learnt from those that knew him, he took care to neglect none of those things which he found in the Gospels and the writings of Apostles and prophets, but to the utmost of his power endeavoured to fulfil them all in his deeds.[45]

The Celts as a whole, Bede said, "earnestly practised such works of piety and chastity as they could learn from the Prophets, the Gospels, and the Apostolic writings."[46]

Much of what the early Celtic Christians believed will seem familiar to modern Christian readers, who are by and large familiar with the basic contents of the Bible. Celtic Christians, for example, believed in the Triune nature of God—that there is only one God, but the Godhead has three Persons: the Father, Son, and Holy Spirit. It is noteworthy that the early Celts didn't expend much energy trying to wrestle with *how* the Trinity works; they simply accepted it as a divine mystery because the Scriptures were so clear about the divinity of Jesus.

The early Celtic Christians also believed the Bible's creation

---

45 Bede. *Complete Historical Works of the Venerable Bede*. Delphi Ancient Classics Book 45. Digital, 2817-2818 on Kindle.

46 Ibid., 2447-2448.

account, taking the Genesis account at face value and teaching that God made the world in six days and rested on the seventh:

> *Celtic cosmological views were based on a literal inter-*
> *pretation of the story of Genesis. The elements which*
> *make up the material universe came into being as the*
> *result of a fiat creation, through the agency of Jesus*
> *Christ and by His power. One of the purposes, stressed*
> *by the commentators, for which the world was brought*
> *into being, was that the character of God might be*
> *learned through a study of it. For instance: "Not less*
> *does the disposition of the elements set forth concerning*
> *God and manifest Him than though it were a teacher*
> *who set forth and preached it with his lips." While it is*
> *true that there was no spoken language through which*
> *nature communicated with men, the Celtic mystic felt*
> *that "without art of learning and practice by anyone,*
> *it is understood in every nation the way in which the*
> *elements sound and show forth the knowledge of God*
> *through the work that they do and the alteration that is*
> *on them." It was probably this appreciation of nature's*
> *revelation of the character of God that led to the produc-*
> *tion of so much beautiful mystic nature poetry.*[47]

Celtic Christians also believed in the power of prayer, just as most modern Christians do. In fact, Patrick was known to pray up to 100 times a day, convinced that his prayers were not falling on deaf ears, but that the Creator God actually heard

---

47 Hardinge, Leslie. *The Celtic Church in Britain*. Brushton, New York: Teach Services, 1995, 59.

him. It was a habit he developed during his years as a slave, and continued throughout the rest of his life:

> *When I came to Ireland I spent each day tending sheep and I prayed many times during the day. Thus I grew more and more in the love of God. And as the fear of God increased in me so did my faith, so that in a single day I would pray up to one hundred times and in the course of the night I would pray nearly as many times again. When I was tending the sheep on mountains and in woods and in the dark before the dawn I would awaken and pray in the snow, in the frost and in the rain. No harm came to me as there was no idleness in me, as I can now see, for my spirit was always fervent.*[48]

As with the 1st-century Christian church, Celtic Christians anticipated a literal return of Christ, which would take place at the culmination of human history:

> *Through Christ all things visible and invisible were made. He was made man, He overcame death, He was received into Heaven by the Father who gave Him all sovereignty over every name in Heaven, on the earth and under the earth, that every tongue should confess His name. For Jesus Christ is Lord and God, in whom we believe and whose coming we await in the near future. He will be Judge of the living and the dead, who*

---

48 *Patrick's Confession*, par. 16. O'Donoghue, Fr. Neil Xavier. *St. Patrick: His Confession and Other Works.* Catholic Book Publishing Corporation. Digital, Kindle.

will reward every man as his deeds deserve and who
will pour out an abundance of the Holy Spirit upon us
as the gift and pledge of immortality.[49]

It is worth noting that in the complete corpus of Celtic Christian writing, there is no mention of a secret return of
Christ, in which Jesus quietly and quickly removes Christians
from the world prior to a final period of tribulation. It was not
until the 19th century that talk of a secret rapture of the church
appeared in Christian literature. The Celts, like most every other
Christian who lived during the first 1,800 years of the church's
existence, simply taught that Jesus will return in glory, at the
culmination of history, when everybody gets their reward.

The Celts also held the Ten Commandments to be the will
and moral law of God, as with most modern Christians. The
reason humanity needs a Savior, they reasoned, is because we
violated God's moral law, which brought death—the wages of
sin—upon us. The only chance sinful human beings have of obtaining salvation is to lay hold of the righteousness of Christ,
our Substitute. Because of Jesus' sacrifice at Calvary, we have the
privilege of accepting forgiveness for sins, and then, through the
power of the living Christ, begin living a new life in which we
order our lives in harmony with God's will.

There are many points of agreement between early Celtic
Christianity and modern biblical Christianity, because of a common source of authority: the Bible. It is only natural that dispa-
rate groups of people who use the revealed Scriptures to instruct
their faith should have similar sets of beliefs. While the church
of continental Europe was struggling with the mistakes it had

---

49   Ibid., par. 4.

made after the rise of Constantine, there was a much different, distinct form of Christianity emerging on a distant island off the west coast of Europe.

But in some ways, the Celts were almost *ahead* of modern Christianity, because they also believed some things that modern Christians are only beginning to discover in the pages of the Bible. For example, following the lead of Bible passages like 1 Timothy 6:16, the Celts taught that only God has natural immortality—only God can live forever by His own strength. The rest of us, they taught, are mortal. We have what might be termed *conditional immortality*, in that it is only granted to the faithful after the return of Christ. Otherwise, sinful human beings are mortal, because we die and do not live forever.

The Celts taught, based on the Scriptures, that the only way for a sinful human being to become immortal is to be forgiven and covered by the blood of Christ. Apart from that, the wages of sin—death—is the final reward for an unrepentant sinner. Curiously, they never spoke of a place of eternal torment, where God tortures sinners throughout the ceaseless ages of eternity.

The reason they didn't teach an eternally burning hell is because they didn't find it in the Bible. Today, modern Christian scholars are just starting to come to the same conclusion: it is entirely possible that our stories of an everlasting place of burning have more to do with ancient pagan tales than the words of the Bible.[50]

There is another curious feature to Celtic Christianity that represents a direct departure from the practice of mainland Christianity after it passed through the filter of Constantine. As Constantine consolidated his power over the Roman Empire,

---

50   The author explores this possibility more fully in *Draining the Styx*.

he had to harmonize two segments of the city's population: the pagans, who were frustrated by Constantine's apparent abandonment of their traditional religion, and the Christians, the religious group to which his mother belonged. The pagans observed the first day of the week in honor of the sun god (which is why the first day of the week is still labeled the "sun day" to the present day), and in an act apparently intended to appease them, Constantine declared the first day of the week to be a day of rest:

> On the venerable Day of the sun let the magistrates and people residing in cities rest, and let all workshops be closed. In the country, however, persons engaged in agriculture may freely and lawfully continue their pursuits: because it often happens that another day is not so suitable for grain-sowing or for vine-planting: lest by neglecting the proper moment for such operations the bounty of heaven should be lost.[51]

The astute reader will note that there is no mention of a Christian Sabbath or the resurrection of Christ in the wording of the decree; that is because the world's first "blue law" had nothing to do with Christianity and everything to do with venerating the sun. In reality, most of the Christian world continued to observe the seventh-day Sabbath on Saturday for many generations after the close of the New Testament canon, knowing nothing of a change to the fourth commandment. Jesus Himself referred to the fact that the Sabbath would still be in effect after

---

51 Codex Justinianus, 3.12.3. Schaff, Philip. *History of the Christian Church*, Vol. 3, 5th Ed. New York: Scribner, 1902, 380.

His return to heaven. Speaking of the Roman sack of Jerusalem in AD 70, Jesus warned his disciples: "Pray that your flight may not be in winter or on the Sabbath." (Matthew 24:20)

But as the Christian church began to assume the reins of power in the west, church councils followed suit with further decrees prohibiting work on Sunday. Eventually, the Sabbath was identified with the Jews, and observing it was referred to as "Judaizing," as in the 29th Canon of the Synod of Laodicea in AD 384:

> Christians must not judaize by resting on the Sabbath, but must work on that day, rather honouring the Lord's Day; and, if they can, resting then as Christians. But if any shall be found to be judaizers, let them be anathema from Christ.[52]

Curiously, the same synod continued to recognize the seventh day of the week as an appropriate day for studying Scripture:

> The Gospels are to be read on the Sabbath [i.e. Saturday], with the other Scriptures.[53]

It was after Constantine that the mainline Christian church of the west began to observe Sunday as "the Lord's Day" and reject the Sabbath of the fourth commandment. Roman Christians seemed willing to make the change; in fact, many of them

---

52 Percival, Henry, trans. Philip Schaff and Henry Wace, eds. *Nicene and Post-Nicene Fathers*, Second Series, Vol. 14. Buffalo, NY: Christian Literature Publishing Co., 1900.

53 Ibid., Canon 16.

had already made the change back in the 2nd century. By accommodating their worship practices to the local pagan festivals, they hoped to distance themselves from the city's Jews—so when Constantine looked for an opportunity to create unity between his pagan and Christian subjects, the observance of the first day of the week seemed like a natural fit.

It offers one more startling piece of evidence that the description of the little horn power in Daniel chapter 7—pointing to the compromise of Christianity—was absolutely correct:

> *"He shall speak pompous words against the Most High, shall persecute the saints of the Most High, and shall intend to change times and law."* (Daniel 7:25)

When Christianity would go off the rails, Daniel predicted, it would attempt to change "times and laws." There is only one item in God's moral law that deals with time: the Sabbath commandment, which requires the observance of the seventh day as the Sabbath and a memorial of creation. It is a commandment that deals specifically with God's right to sit on the throne of the universe, since His authority is derived from His status as Creator:

> *"You are worthy, O Lord, to receive glory and honor and power; for You created all things, and by Your will they exist and were created."* (Revelation 4:11)

It may explain the curious practice of Celtic Christians, who knew nothing of the radical changes taking place in Rome. Patrick lived and worked 400 years after Christ, in an environment isolated from the official Christianity of the Dark Ages.

Which day did Patrick observe? Patrick's letters indicate that an angel visited him many times, and *almost always on the seventh day of the week.*

There is another reference to observance of the seventh-day Sabbath in a letter attributed to Columbanus, another famous Celtic missionary who lived almost 200 years *after* Patrick:

> *We are bidden to work on six days, but on the seventh, which is the Sabbath, we are restrained from every servile labour. Now by the number six the completeness of our work is meant, since it was in six days the Lord made heaven and earth. Yet on the Sabbath we are forbidden to labour at any servile work, that is sin, since he who commits sin is a slave to sin, so that, when in this present age we have completely fulfilled our works, not hardening our hearts, we may deserve to reach that true rest, which is denied to the unruly, as the Lord says through David, If they shall enter into my rest.*[54]

Toward the end of the 6th century, Pope Gregory the Great started sending monks to live in Britain. They inevitably came in contact with the Celtic missionaries, who were already proselytizing in the rest of Europe from their bases in the British Isles. The Roman monks were baffled by what they found: the Celts, while clearly Christian, did not believe as the Roman monks had been taught. A report was sent back to Rome:

---

54   *Columbini Opera*, 203. In Hardinge, 83.

- The Celts allowed their priests to marry.

- They were practicing an older form of immersion baptism, in which the candidate was completely submerged beneath the water.

- They knew nothing of Roman canon law.

- They had their own translation of the Bible.

- They kept Saturday as a day of rest.

The monks discovered there was another form of Christianity, one that had grown up outside the reach of the Roman Empire, and because it only had the Bible as its authoritative source, it more closely resembled the church of the New Testament. As the Western world plunged into its darkest hour, a brand-new Christian church just "happened" to emerge in one of the world's most remote places—a church that answers to the description found in the book of Revelation:

> *But the woman was given two wings of a great eagle, that she might fly into the wilderness to her place, where she is nourished for a time and times and half a time, from the presence of the serpent.* (Revelation 12:14)

The miraculous conversion of the Celts is one of the most incredible untold stories in Christian history. What is even more incredible is the story of how we got from Patrick to Martin Luther.

CHAPTER SEVEN:
THE VOICE OF THE MARTYRS

When He opened the fifth seal, I saw under the altar the souls of those who had been slain for the word of God and for the testimony which they held. And they cried with a loud voice, saying, "How long, O Lord, holy and true, until You judge and avenge our blood on those who dwell on the earth?" (Revelation 6:9, 10)

PATRICK'S RETURN TO IRELAND REVOLUTIONIZED the Irish people, liberating them from bloodthirsty pagan deities and introducing them to a God whose love was so profound that He gave His own life to save them. Their passion for wild, extravagant living was channeled into a new passion to share the gospel with others. In addition to becoming guardians of the world's great literature, the Celts also became incredibly effective missionaries.

Irish monks lived communally, in humble abbeys. When a monastic settlement grew too large, a number of the monks would leave to establish a new missionary center elsewhere. In short order, their centers of learning spilled over the boundaries of Hibernia and across the water to the rest of the British Isles and continental Europe—to the extent that when Charlemagne sat on the throne of the Holy Roman Empire in the 8th century, he knew the work and teachings of Irish monks. In fact, he knew of more than 600 monasteries the Irish had built in his own territory. Author Derek Wilson describes the impact Celtic Christianity had on the rest of Europe:

> *Two religious currents—one from the north and one from the south—washed over Francia. Celtic spirituality was, and is, a very distinctive strain of religious experience. The conditions for its development and spread were restricted in both space and time. Like a diamond formed under intense pressure, it developed in a narrow cultural stratum sandwiched between the ancient rock of Celtic paganism and the new deposits of Anglo-Saxon paganism. The first native, British Christians built centers for the exercise of their highly disciplined routines of worship and meditation in the remoter parts of the remotest western province of what had been the Roman Empire. In the white heat of a spiritual commitment that refused to be obsessed with mere survival, they planned and launched ever more extensive evangelistic crusades. This, the first experience of Britain at the heart of Europe, was one of the most remarkable phases in the long history of Christian missionary endeavor, and its legends ring with the names of such heroes as Patrick, Columba, Aidan, Columban and Boniface. Most religious revivals peter out after a few decades. This one lasted in full vigor for an amazing four centuries, from the time when the last Roman conquerors departed to the moment when the first Viking invaders*

arrived. It would be impossible to overestimate the long-term effects of this religious explosion.[55]

At the beginning of the 6th century, about 100 years after Patrick first evangelized Hibernia, an Irish monk—a prince who chose to enter the monastic life—found work as a copyist at Clonary Abbey. His name was Columcille, or Columba to the English. He had been assigned the task of copying an exquisitely beautiful psalter, and became so enamored with the book that he decided to make a copy for himself.

The abbot, Finian, discovered what he had done, and confiscated his personal copy. Columba was required to stand trial before King Diarmait, the High King of Ireland, who ruled (in what may be the world's first copyright case) that making unauthorized personal copies of books was a form of theft. He would not be permitted to keep it.

The verdict gave birth to a deep grudge against the king in Columba's heart. In later years, when the same king had one of Columba's followers killed, Columba sensed an opportunity. The death of a monk was a grave injustice, he insisted, and must be avenged. He mobilized a number of his own men, went to war against the high king, and won decisively. More than 3,000 of the king's men died—3,001, to be exact.

Now instead of making a copy, Columba helped himself to the original psalter. When the rest of the Celtic church found out what he had done, however, they protested loudly. Columba was banished from Ireland, and told he could never come back unless he made up for what he had done by baptizing as many people as he had killed: 3,001.

55   Wilson, Derek. *Charlemagne*. New York: Vintage Books, 2005, 17.

In about the year AD 564, about 100 years after the death of Patrick, Columba took 12 of his followers, as all good Irish monks did when they meant to start a new abbey, and he set sail for the island of Iona, just off the coast of Scotland. Iona was just far enough away that he could no longer see the Irish coast.

It was roughly 90 years after the collapse of the Western Roman Empire, and there were very few Romans left in Northern Europe. Most of them had returned home, leaving a massive vacuum in the British Isles which the Germanic tribes from the European mainland—distant relatives to the Goths—were only too happy to fill: Anglo-Saxons, Frisians, and others began to pour over the English Channel and settle in the abandoned Roman province of Britannia. Among the illiterate barbarian settlers were people with a desire for learning—and they soon heard of the wise and learned Celts.

Because of the influx of foreigners, at least in part, the new abbey at Iona became a great center of learning. From this remote spot, perched on the edge of the world, Celtic Christians sent hundreds—possibly *thousands*—of missionaries back to the European continent to establish even more centers of learning. By the time Columba died, he had managed to build 60 such centers of learning (that we know of), and as noted earlier, by the time Charlemagne came to power as the Holy Roman Emperor at the beginning of the 9th century, there were more than 600 Celtic evangelistic centers across Western Europe.

Did Columba ever baptize 3,001 people? Without a doubt, the number was much larger.

Another early Celtic missionary worth noting is Columbanus, who was in his mid-20s when Columba was exiled to Scotland. He was trained as a missionary in Bangor, and around the year AD 590—at about the age of 50—he also assembled 12 followers and set out for distant lands, this time in mainland Europe. He managed to establish another 60 monasteries in France, Germany, Switzerland, and over the Alps into northern Italy. One of his most famous settlements was Bobbio, in Italy, a community Columbanus built in his 70s that still exists to this day.

That means, of course, that a biblical form of Christianity not only survived the period of the pale horse on the fringes of the empire, but it also made its way to Italy, to the very gates of the city where the Constantinian compromise had first taken place. The first time the Celts came to Rome, they brought destruction; the next time they arrived, nearly a millennium later, they brought the gospel. The first time, they defeated Rome; the second time, they defied her.

The Celts were not alone in preserving biblical Christianity. We know of many groups that lived outside the boundaries of Rome, ranging from North Africa to the Far East, many of which also practiced a primitive form of Christianity. Many of the same curious practices were found in these other "outsider" Christian groups, including a high regard for Scripture and observing the seventh-day Sabbath.

But *inside* the Roman Empire, not far from Columbanus' settlement at Bobbio in northern Italy, there was another group of Christians who emerged in isolation from the great compromise launched by Constantine. This group, the Waldenses, was not protected by the remoteness of a distant island, but by the nearly inaccessible mountain passes of the Alps. While the Celtic Christians were tragically absorbed into mainstream Christianity after many centuries, the Waldenses persisted for a much longer time.

The origin of these incredible people is veiled in a bit of mystery. The official line given by most encyclopedic sources is that they were founded by Peter Waldo, a wealthy merchant from Lyons who, in about the year 1170, suddenly became convicted that God would have him dispense with his wealth and use his talents to help the poor. He launched a movement, teaching people the art of self-denial for the sake of the gospel, and his followers were named after him: the Waldensians.

It's a nice story, and you'll still find it plastered all over the internet—but it couldn't possibly be true. The distinctive groups of believers found in the hidden recesses of the Alps have gone by many names over the years—Waldenses, Valdenses, Waldensians, Vaudois—and those names appear in the historical record many years before Peter Waldo. There is little doubt that Waldo was associated with the Waldenses after his conversion experience, but the phonetic similarity with his surname is mere coincidence.

The historian Alexis Muston, writing in the 19th century, explains where the Waldenses got their name:

> It is, however, from their character as dalesmen, or men of the valleys, that they have received their name. This name, derived primarily from the Latin vallis, a valley, is variously spelled. The French form of the word, which is val, gives rise to a plural vaux, and thence to the adjective Vaudois. The Italian form of the word gives the adjective Vallenses, strengthened into Valdenses, and thence corrupted in English into Waldenses.[56]

---

56 Muston, Alexis. *The Waldenses: Sketches of the Evangelical Christians of the Valleys of Piedmont.* Philadelphia: Presbyterian Board of Publication, 1853, 18.

The Waldenses, then, were simply the "people of the valleys," a broad group of believers who lived in the mountains on the border between Italy and France—a group that endured repeated persecution from the official state church over the centuries because of their distinctive beliefs. The idea that they did not appear on the timeline of history until the end of the 12th century is untenable; a number of their key writings, in fact—works like the *Noble Lesson* (1100), *Catechism* (1100), and *Antichrist* (1120) predate Peter Waldo by at least half a century.

To determine how the Waldenses came to exist requires a little bit of detective work, because many of their records were destroyed when persecutors set fire to a key Waldensian library in the 16th century (approximately 1559). There is enough remaining data, however, to piece together a fascinating story.

One theory suggests that the Vaudois were early Christians who fled the city of Rome during the brutal persecutions brought on by the pagan empire during the 1st and 2nd centuries. As they fled to the north, they found refuge in the remote valleys of the Piedmont region and continued to believe and live as 1st-century Christians did for many long centuries. In favor of this theory is the unique Latin Bible used by the Waldenses known as the *Italic*. It predates Jerome's Vulgate edition by more than two centuries, created in AD 157, and uses a form of Latin that existed during the Roman persecution of Christians. (Curiously, it was also the version that many of the Celtic missionaries used and brought with them to Columbanus' settlement in Bobbio. Of course, that might also suggest that the Waldenses inherited the Italic version *from* the Celts at some point in the 7th century, but that would still establish the origin of the Waldensian church more than 500 years before Peter Waldo.)

A second theory is deeply intriguing. In the 15th chapter of his letter to the Romans, Paul writes:

> But now no longer having a place in these parts, and having a great desire these many years to come to you, whenever I journey to Spain, I shall come to you. For I hope to see you on my journey, and to be helped on my way there by you, if first I may enjoy your company for a while. But now I am going to Jerusalem to minister to the saints. For it pleased those from Macedonia and Achaia to make a certain contribution for the poor among the saints who are in Jerusalem. It pleased them indeed, and they are their debtors. For if the Gentiles have been partakers of their spiritual things, their duty is also to minister to them in material things. Therefore, when I have performed this and have sealed to them this fruit, I shall go by way of you to Spain. (Romans 15:23-28)

The Scriptures are silent on whether or not Paul ever succeeded in making the journey to Spain, but the writings of early Christians suggest that he did. The Muratorian Fragment is a document found in the Ambrosian Library in Milan, and originally comes from the library at Columbanus' monastery at Bobbio. Because it mentions "The Shepherd of Hermas," an apocryphal New Testament book, as a recent composition, it is believed to be a copy of material that dates back to the 2nd century. Speaking of Luke's gospel, the document reads:

> For "most excellent Theophilus" Luke compiled the individual events that took place in his presence—as

he plainly shows by omitting the martyrdom of Peter as
well as the departure of Paul from the city [of Rome]
when he journeyed to Spain.[57]

One of the earliest Christian documents outside of the
New Testament is a letter from Clement, Bishop of Rome, to the
church in Corinth, believed to date back to the end of the 1st
century, or at the latest, the beginning of the 2nd century. There
is some thought that the author of the letter may have been the
Clement mentioned by Paul in Philippians 4:3 as a "fellow work-
er," and if that is true, Clement would have been in a position to
know something of Paul. He writes:

Through envy Paul, too, showed by example the prize
that is given to patience: seven times was he cast into
chains; he was banished; he was stoned; having become
a herald, both in the East and in the West, he obtained
the noble renown due to his faith; and having preached
righteousness to the whole world, and having come to
the extremity of the West, and having borne witness
before rulers, he departed at length out of the world,
and went to the holy place, having become the greatest
example of patience. (1 Clement 5:5-7)[58]

While the letter does not specifically mention Spain, it does
mention a trip to "the extremity of the West," which certainly does match Spain's position in the Mediterranean basin. In

---

57 An English translation of the Muratorian Fragment can be found at
www.bible-researcher.com/muratorian.html

58 Charles Hoole Translation, 1885.

the late 4th century (or possibly the very early 5th century), during the years in which Rome was beginning to crumble and Ireland was preparing to receive the gospel, John Chrysostom, the Archbishop of Constantinople, preached a sermon series on the book of 2 Timothy. In the 10th sermon, he offhandedly remarked that Paul had been to Spain:

> *"Trophimus I have left at Miletum sick." Miletus was near Ephesus. Did this happen then when he sailed to Judea, or upon some other occasion? For after he had been in Rome, he returned to Spain, but whether he came thence again into these parts, we know not.*[59]

Even though Paul left no personal record of a successful trip to Spain, the early Christian church certainly seems to remember that he had been there. Why is this important to the Waldensian story? If Paul had made the journey from Rome to Spain on land, he would have had to pass through the Piedmont region—precisely the place where the Vaudois church emerged.

The Waldensians themselves remember that their roots are very ancient, and likely date back to apostolic times. Writing in the 19th century, historian Alexis Muston describes the likelihood of a very early genesis for the Vaudois church:

> *Their own account of the matter uniformly has been that their religion has descended with them from father to son by uninterrupted succession from the time of the apostles. There certainly is no improbability in the con-*

---

59 The entire sermon can be found at www.ccel.org/ccel/schaff/
npnf113.v.iv.x.html

jecture that the gospel was preached to them by some of those early missionaries who carried Christianity into Gaul. The common passage from Rome to Gaul at that time lay directly through the Cottian Alps, and Gaul we know received the gospel early in the second century at the latest, probably before the close of the first century. If the apostle Paul ever made that "journey into Spain," (Rom. xv. 28,) which he speaks of in his epistle to the Romans, and in which he proposed to go by way of Rome, his natural route would have been in the same direction, and it is not impossible that his voice was actually heard among those retired valleys. The most common opinion among Protestant writers is, that the conversion of the Waldenses was begun by some of the very early Christian missionaries, perhaps by some of the apostles themselves, on their way to Gaul, and that it was completed and the churches more fully organized by a large influx of Christians from Rome, after the first general persecution of Nero. The Christians of Rome, scattered by this terrible event, would naturally flee from the plain country to the mountains, carrying with them the gospel and its institutions.

Such is the opinion of Henry Arnaud, one of the most intelligent of the Waldensian pastors. "Neither has their church ever been reformed," says Arnaud, "whence arises its title of evangelic. The Waldenses are in fact descended from those refugees from Italy, who, after St. Paul had there preached the gospel, abandoned their beautiful country, and fled, like the woman mentioned

in the Apocalypse, to these wild mountains, where they
have, to this day, handed down the gospel from father to
son, in the same purity and simplicity as it was preached
by St. Paul."[60]

Document after document that survived the attempted
purge of the Waldenses asserts that they have existed in the
Piedmont region from very ancient times, and that their Christian beliefs have been handed down through the generations
from apostolic times. The suggestion, then, that they were disciples of Peter Waldo, only existing as a church after 1170, is very
hard to reconcile with the existing record.

In a report written for the Inquisition by Reinerius Saccho
in the middle of the 13th century, he refers to the Waldensians
as "Leonists" because of a rumor that the sect was started by
a man named Leo in the time of Constantine. He enumerates
three reasons he considered the Waldensians to be dangerous:

There is no sect so dangerous as the Leonists, for three
reasons: first, it is the most ancient—some say as old as
Sylvester, others as the apostles themselves. Secondly, it
is very generally disseminated: there is no country where
it has not gained some footing. Thirdly, while other sects
are profane and blasphemous, this retains the utmost
show of piety; they live justly before men, and believe
nothing respecting God which is not good.[61]

---

60 Muston, 28-29.

61 Waddington, George. *A History of the Church—From the Earliest Ages to*
    the Reformation. Digital, 12351-12354 on Kindle.

Jonathan Edwards, the great revival preacher of the 18th century, made this comment about the Waldenses in his *History of the Work of Redemption*:

> *Besides these particular persons dispersed, there was a certain people called the Waldenses, who lived separate from all the rest of the world. . . . The place where they dwelt was the Vaudois, or the five valleys of Piedmont, a very mountainous country, between Italy and France; it was compassed about with those exceeding high mountains, the Alps, which were almost impassable, and therefore the valleys were almost inaccessible. There this people lived for many ages, in a state of a separation from all the world, having very little to do with any other people. And there they served God in the ancient purity of his worship. . . .*
>
> *One of the Popish writers, speaking of the Waldenses, says, "The heresy of the Waldenses is the oldest heresy in the world. It is supposed that they first betook themselves to this place among the mountains, to hide themselves from the severity of the heathen persecutions which existed before Constantine the Great."*[62]

While the precise origin of the Waldenses has been lost in the murk of history, two things are clear: (1) the Waldenses have very old roots, and (2) the mainline state church considered them heretical and wanted them eliminated. One can't help

---

62 Edwards, Jonathan. *A History of the Work of Redemption*. Worcester, MA: Isaiah Thomas and Leonard Worcester, 1792, 267.

but wonder what these people believed that made them seem a threat to the growing church-state alliance.

At a time when owning a personal copy of the Bible was often considered a capital crime, the Waldenses spent long days making copies by hand, just as the Celts had done. While the Celts were sheltered by their remote distance from Rome, however, the Waldensians were carrying out their missionary endeavors in Rome's backyard. They hid fragments of the Bible in their clothing, and posing as traveling merchants, they presented the copies to interested parties across Western Europe. Some have estimated that at their peak of activity, the Waldensian missionaries were able to travel from Cologne to Florence and stay in the home of a convert every single night.

The various Waldensian communities met annually for a synod at Angrogna, where the business of the church was discussed. Across the Piedmont region, it is estimated that they had around 150 pastors, known as *barbas,* shepherding their congregations. In order to become a *barba,* however, you had to prove your evangelistic ability: only those who had spent at least three years in the mission field were considered for the posts. The missionary fervor of the Waldensians was such that the number of missionaries always greatly outpaced the number of pastors.

Like the Celts, they were mission-minded, and consumed by a passion to share the Scriptures and Christ. Their motto was *Lux Lucet in Tenebris:* "Light shines in darkness." They understood that the Western Roman Empire had fallen on very hard times, and that darkness had spread across Christendom in the wake of Constantine's compromise. They were resolved to maintain a biblical Christianity, and it was this feature that made them an object of resentment among the elites of the established church.

Their beliefs, like those of the Celts, ring true for many modern Christians, but were considered problematic to many of our ancestors who had fallen under the spell of the Dark Ages. Their beliefs included:

1. **A belief in the Bible as the authoritative rule of faith for the church.** The Waldenses rejected the addition of tradition to Scripture as authoritative for faith. Their Bible contained the same Old Testament canon accepted by the Jews, and they rejected the additional books that made their way into some canonical books later in the 16th century. "We read them for the instruction of the people," their Confession of Faith reads, "but not to confirm the authority of the doctrines of the church."[63]

For the Waldenses to accept a Christian doctrine, they had to find it clearly laid out in the Bible.

The great church historian, Augustus Neander, elaborates on their love for Scripture:

> *As the origin of the Waldenses is to be traced to the reading of the Bible, they always remained true to this direction. A great knowledge of the Bible distinguished men and women among them; and this circumstance, contrasted with the ignorance of the Scriptures among*

---

63   Confession of Faith, Article III. In Antoine Monastier, *A History of the Vaudois Church from Its Origin and of the Vaudois of Piedmont to the Present Day.* London: Religious Tract Society, 1848, 83.

the clergy, contributed to their spread. Rainer[64] *reckons among the means which served to promote the sect, the translation of the Old and New Testaments into the spoken language of the country. The same writer mentions in this connection, that he had seen an illiterate peasant who had learned by heart the book of Job, and several others who had committed the entire New Testament.*[65]

2. **A simple understanding of the gospel.** Article IV of their Confession reads, "God formed Adam in His image and in his likeness; but through the malice of the devil, and by Adam's disobedience, sin entered into the world, and all are sinners in Adam and by Adam." Article VII states, "We believe that Christ is to us life, truth, peace, and righteousness, Shepherd and Advocate, Sacrifice and Priest; that he died for the salvation of all believers, and rose again for our justification." (Thus it is also evident that they believed in the bodily resurrection of Christ.) The Waldenses were clear that the only path to salvation is the atoning death of Christ at the cross, and that works—while important for displaying the changed nature of the sinner's heart—were not a path to earning salvation.[66] They emphasize that only God (and not the clergy) can forgive sins.

---

64 This is the anglicized name of the Inquisitor Reinerius Saccho, mentioned previously.

65 Neander, Augustus. Torrey, Joseph, trans. *General History of the Christian Religion and Church.* London: Henry G. Bohn, 1852, 360.

66 Ibid., 85.

3. **A belief that God does not require stately cathedrals and other grandiose institutions in order to hear your prayers.** It was often said among the Waldenses that God could hear prayer from a barn just as well as He could hear prayer from a church. They generally eschewed elaborate living and were widely known for simplicity and modesty. *The Noble Lesson*, a document dated as early as 1100, emphasizes Paul's determination to be content with food and clothing. (1 Timothy 6:8)

4. **A rejection of rites and rituals not found in the Bible.** While the mainstream church of Western Europe was adding many new requirements to the practice of the Christian faith, the Waldensian Confession stated, "We have always believed that all things invented by men, such as the feasts and vigils of the saints, holy water, abstinence on certain days from meat and other kinds of food . . . ought not to be mentioned in the presence of God." [67] Holy water, said the Vaudois, was no more special than rainwater. Pilgrimages to holy sites, they claimed, did little besides consume your savings. And the relics of the saints, which were mostly body parts, were nothing more than rotting flesh.

5. **An understanding that the prophecies of the Bible identified corruption within Christianity as a key problem.** The Waldenses understood that the beast power of Revelation 13 was not an outsider, but a tragic description of Christianity itself as it compromised in the centuries following the establishment of the church. In *The Noble Lesson*, the author states:

---

67 *Confession*, Articles X, XI.

*Such is the man: accomplished in sin, he exalts himself
above all that is called God, and that is worshipped; he
is opposed to all truth, and is seated in the temple of
God, that is, in the church, making himself to be God; he
comes with all sorts of seductions for those that perish.*[68]

6. **A dedication to a godly lifestyle**. They were widely known
   to be Christ-like in their deportment, a fact that even their
   enemies could not deny. You will remember that the report
   Reinerius Saccho filed with the Inquisition deemed the
   Waldenses especially dangerous because they "retain(ed) the
   utmost show of piety; they live justly before men, and believe
   nothing respecting God which is not good."

7. **An understanding of the Great Commission of Matthew
   28, and an unstoppable passion for evangelistic mission.** This much is evident from the historical record: the
   Waldenses were willing to suffer centuries of privation and
   persecution in order to remain faithful to the call of Christ
   to "make disciples of all the nations." Few Christians, apart
   from the Celts, were as successful as the Vaudois in carrying
   out the Gospel Commission in Medieval Europe.

Many of the missionaries worked as traveling merchants,
selling luxuries from the East such as silk and pearls. They
would hide fragments of the Bible in their clothing, and when
a customer seemed interested in spiritual matters, they would
literally risk their lives to present them with a copy of Scripture. Historian Augustus Neander describes their method:

---

68   Monastier, 77.

Though in general they supported themselves by manual labor rather than by trade, and scattered themselves more among the people than among the nobles, yet a number of them dealt in jewels and ornaments of dress as a means of obtaining access to the families of the great. When they had disposed of rings and trinkets, and were asked if they had nothing more to sell, they answered, "Yes, we have jewels still more precious than any you have seen; we would be glad to show you these also, if you would promise not to betray us to the clergy." On being assured that they should be safe, they said, "We have a precious stone, so brilliant, that by its light a man may see God; another, which radiates such a fire as to enkindle the love of God in the heart of its possessor"—and so they went on. The precious stones which they meant were passages of the Holy Scriptures in their various applications.[69]

A stirring poem written in the 19th century by an admirer of the Waldenses illustrates their merchant-missionary spirit beautifully:

The Vaudois Missionary
*"O, lady fair, these silks of mine
Are beautiful and rare—
The richest web of the Indian loom
Which beauty's self might wear.
And these pearls are pure and mild to behold,
And with radiant light they vie;
I have brought them with me a weary way:
Will my gentle lady buy?"*

---

69   Neander, Vol. 8, 361.

And the lady smiled on the worn old man,
Through the dark and clustering curls
Which veiled her brow as she bent to view
His silk and glittering pearls;
And she placed their price in the old man's hand,
And lightly turned away:
But she paused at the wanderer's earnest call—
"My gentle lady, stay!"

"O, lady fair, I have yet a gem
Which a purer lustre flings
Than the diamond flash of the jewelled crown
On the lofty brow of kings;
A wonderful pearl of exceeding price,
Whose virtue shall not decay;
Whose light shall be as a spell to thee,
And a blessing on thy way!"

The lady glanced at the mirroring steel,
Where her youthful form was seen,
Where her eyes shone clear and her dark locks waved
Their clasping pearls between;
"Bring forth thy pearl of exceeding worth,
Thou traveller gray and old;
And name the price of thy precious gem,
And my pages shall count thy gold."

The cloud went off from the pilgrim's brow,
As a small and meagre book
Unchased with gold or diamond gem,
From his folding robe he took:
"Here, lady fair, is the pearl of price—
May it prove as such to thee!
Nay, keep they gold—I ask it not—
For the Word of God is free."

The hoary traveller went his way—
But the gift he left behind
Hath had its pure and perfect work
On that high-born maiden's mind;
And she hath turned from her pride of sin
To the lowliness of truth,
And given her new-born heart to God
In its beautiful hour of youth.

And she hath left the old gray walls
Where an evil faith hath power,
The courtly knights of her father's train,
And the maidens of her bower;
And she hath gone to the Vaudois vale,
By lordly feet untrod,
Where the poor and needy of earth are rich
In the perfect love of God![70]

There is another intriguing possibility that might tie Waldensian beliefs to those of the Celts: it is possible, as with Patrick and Columba, that some of them observed the seventh-day Sabbath. Given their reliance on Scripture as the sole authority, it is not unreasonable to search for evidence that they might have. It should be noted that the idea is not widely accepted, even among some historians within the modern Waldensian church.

There is enough evidence, however, to certainly open the door to the possibility. What makes many students of Waldensian history suspect that there were indeed Sabbatarians among the Vaudois are the curious nicknames they were given: *Sabbati, Sabbatati,* and *Insabbatati.* The etymological similarity to the word "Sabbath" is hard to miss.

70   Anonymous. In Muston, 44.

There are three major theories as to why people began using these names for the Waldenses:

1. Some say that they were so named because of their refusal to observe the feast days prescribed by the church in Rome. The word "*In*sabbatati," proponents of this theory claim, suggests that they were *not* keeping the "sabbaths" of the mainstream church, which would include things like saints' days.

2. There is another old theory that suggests the nicknames came as a result of the sandals or wooden shoes the Waldenses wore. This is the reason proposed by many religious encyclopedias:

   Their practice of wearing sandals or wooden shoes (sabots) caused them to be named "Sandaliati," "Insabbatati," "Sabbatati," "Sabotiers." [71]

The theory suggests that the Waldenses identified themselves by placing a mark on their shoes, but as 18th-century historian Robert Robinson points out, it seems improbable:

Is it likely, that people, who could not descend from their mountains into neighbouring states without hazarding their lives through the furious zeal of inquisitors, should tempt danger by affixing a visible mark on their shoes? Beside, the shoe of the peasants happens to be famous in this country, it was of a different fashion, and was called Abarca.[72]

---

71 www.newadvent.org/cathen/15527b.htm

72 Robinson, Robert. *Ecclesiastical Researches*. Cambridge: Francis Hodson, 1792, 304.

He raises a good point: why would a heavily persecuted people make life harder by wearing a visible mark to distinguish them from the rest of the population? It doesn't make sense, given the way the Waldenses are known to have operated: by posing as merchants and secreting copies of Scripture in the folds of their clothes until the right opportunity presented itself.

Robinson further suggests that the nickname was simply a corruption of a Latin word referring to the mountain country from which the Vaudois hailed. He also points out a Vaudois believer in the records who went by the name of John Zapata. His reasoning, while plausible, seems less than satisfactory to this author, because it seems to involve too many etymological leaps to be credible:

> The Latin word capui, *a head, was corrupted by the Spaniards into* cabeça, *and hence came* cabo, *a cape, a headland. They called these people* los incabats, *and founded the word* enzabats, *meaning inhabitants of the hills, mountaineers. By a little crook, which they called* cedilla, *placed under the letter c, they inform the reader that it is to be sounded like an s or a z.*[73]

It is certainly true that words morph significantly over time, and take many forms as they pass from language to language as we have already seen in the transformation of *Vaudois* to *Waldensian*. But in this case, perhaps Occam's Razor[74] is correct.

---

73 Ibid., 304.

74 A principle first stated by William of Ockham in the 14th century, which suggests that when you are faced with several possible explanations for something in the realm of science, the simplest is probably the truth.

The biblically-minded character of these people, combined with the rather striking similarity of the nicknames to the word *sabbath*, suggests that it is at least likely that Sabbath-keepers were to be found among the Waldensians.

Melchior Goldast, the noted historian and Swiss jurist, writing in the early 17th century, certainly believed it:

> *They were called* Insabbatati, *not because they were circumcized, but because they kept the Jewish Sabbath.*[75]

What we do know for certain is that the beliefs of the Waldenses differed enough from the official mainline church-state doctrine that they endured unbelievable persecution as a result, much more than did the Celts, whose relative isolation and early historical appearance likely spared them much of the suffering heaped on the Waldenses.

Their wild evangelistic success angered the prelates of mainstream Christianity. The Vaudois' refusal to acknowledge the Bishop of Rome as anything but one minister among equals flew in the face of the claims put forth by the church for centuries. Their further insistence that God does not require ornate buildings, nor does He make people pay to emancipate their relatives from purgatory, threatened to throw cold water on a very successful fundraising program.

The Waldenses were officially denounced as a threat to the Mother Church, and in 1184, at the Synod of Verona, they were officially excommunicated. Excommunication did little to dampen Waldensian evangelistic fervor, so in 1487, Inno-

---

75   Robinson, 303, Note 10.

cent VIII issued a papal bull, calling for the *extermination* of the Waldenses, after which they were ruthlessly persecuted—almost to the brink of extinction.

The horrific events that followed are not for the weak of heart. At various times, the Waldenses had their lands confiscated, and they were subjected to public humiliation, burned the stake, hunted like wild animals, and slaughtered by the thousands. "There is no town in Piedmont, under a Waldensian pastor, where some of the brethren have not been put to death," writes Alexis Muston.[76]

A few examples will suffice to demonstrate how much the organized state church despised the humble Vaudois believers.

In 1545, Francis I, king of France, ordered the destruction of the Waldenses living in the city of Mérindol. He was alarmed by their widespread success outside of the Piedmont Valley, and when he received fabricated reports that they were undermining the stability of his kingdom, he ordered his troops to descend on the city:

> *During the winter of 1544-5 alarming reports of Vaudois activities, deliberately coloured by Oppède to suggest sedition on their part, began to reach the ears of the king and his ministers. On 1 January 1545, therefore, Francis ordered the Arrêt de Mérindol to be carried out. . . .*
>
> *On 11 April Oppède and Polin held a council of war at Marseilles, and a week later operations against the*

---

76   Muston, 87.

Vaudois began. Five villages owned by the dame de Central (who had allegedly refused her daughter's hand to one of Oppède's relatives) were the first to be pillaged and put to the sword. The male inhabitants were either butchered or sent to the galleys, and their womenfolk raped. Another five villages were destroyed, though no massacres took place there, as the inhabitants had fled. Oppède and Polin then turned their attention to Mérindol, where they had expected the Vaudois to make a stand. Instead they found a young imbecile, who was interrogated and shot, and a crowd of women who had taken refuge in the church. These were dragged out and made to suffer every sort of cruelty and indignity. At Cabriéres Oppède and Polin met with some resistance, so they bombarded the village. The defenders surrendered in exchange for their lives, but as they came into the open they were butchered or taken prisoner and sold as slaves.

The number of victims of the Vaudois massacre is not known exactly. Contemporary estimates vary widely: some say hundreds, others thousands. According to the emperor, between 6,000 and 8,000 were killed, including 700 women who were burnt in a church. Another report put the number of survivors sent to the galleys at Marseilles at 666, including young children and men in their eighties; of this total, about 200 died of hunger and exposure.[77]

---

77 Knecht, R. J. *Francis I*. New York: Cambridge University Press, 1982, 405.

In 1655, Charles Emmanuel, the Duke of Savoy, ordered the Waldenses in his territory to start attending mass or return to their ancestral homeland in the mountains. They were given 20 days to comply, and most of them chose to leave even though winter was in full force, and the weather in the mountains would be a death sentence to the sick and elderly.

Jean Léger, a Waldensian pastor who insisted on the ancient origins of his people, noted that of nearly 2,000 congregants in his care, none chose to the offer of compromise. He writes:

> "I was their pastor for eleven years, and I knew every one of them by name; judge, reader, whether I had not cause to weep for joy, as well as for sorrow, when I saw that all the fury of these wolves was not able to influence one of these lambs, and that no earthly advantage could shake their constancy. And when I marked the traces of their blood on the snow and ice over which they had dragged their lacerated limbs, had I not cause to bless God that I had seen accomplished in their poor bodies what remained of the measure of the sufferings of Christ, and especially when I beheld this heavy cross borne by them with a fortitude so noble?"[78]

The Waldensians of the Piedmont welcomed the refugees with open arms, but the worst was yet to come. When it became clear that he had failed to convince the Waldensians to abandon their doctrines, Charles Emmanuel sent troops into the

---

78   Wylie, James. *The History of the Waldenses: Their Victories and Labors.* Digital, 1853-1857 on Kindle.

Waldensian valleys and ordered the locals to house them. The soldiers were to lie in wait until they were signalled to slaughter the Waldenses wholesale. The signal came at 4 a.m. on April 24. Not happy to make a quick end of the Vaudois, the soldiers became coldly cruel. What occurred is not easy reading:

> From the awful narration of Leger, we select only a few instances; but even these few, however mildly stated, grow, without our intending it, into a group of horrors. Little children were torn from the arms of their mothers, clasped by their tiny feet, and their heads dashed against the rocks; or were held between two soldiers and their quivering limbs torn up by main force. Their mangled bodies were then thrown on the highways or fields, to be devoured by beasts. The sick and the aged were burned alive in their dwellings. Some had their hands and arms and legs lopped off, and fire applied to the severed parts to staunch the bleeding and prolong their suffering. Some were flayed alive, some were roasted alive, some disembowelled; or tied to trees in their own orchards, and their hearts cut out. Some were horribly mutilated, and of others the brains were boiled and eaten by these cannibals. Some were fastened down into the furrows of their own fields, and ploughed into the soil as men plough manure into it. Others were buried alive. Fathers were marched to death with the heads of their sons suspended round their necks. Parents were compelled to look on while their children were first outraged, then massacred, before being themselves permitted to die. But here we must stop. We cannot proceed farther

in Leger's awful narration. There come vile, abomina-
ble, and monstrous deeds, utterly and overwhelmingly
disgusting, horrible and fiendish, which we dare not
transcribe.[79]

The slaughter was so unbelievable that it moved the English
poet John Milton to tears:

Avenge, O Lord, thy slaughter'd saints, whose bones
  Lie scattered on the Alpine mountains cold,
  Ev'n them who kept thy truth so pure of old,
  When all our fathers worshipp'd stocks and stones,
Forget not: in thy book record their groans
  Who were thy sheep and in their ancient fold
  Slain by the bloody Piemontese that roll'd
  Mother with infant down the rocks. Their moans
The vales redoubl'd to the hills, and they
  To Heav'n. Their martyr'd blood and ashes sow
  O'er all th' Italian fields where still doth sway
The triple tyrant: that from these may grow
  A hundred-fold, who having learnt thy way
  Early may fly the Babylonian woe.[80]

One last story bears mentioning, and then the case will
have been thoroughly made that the plight of the Waldenses was
an awful one. In 1488, an army of 18,000 men, which was 20

---

79   Ibid., 1925-1935.

80   Milton, John. "On the Late Massacre in Piedmont." *The Complete Poetry
     and Essential Prose of John Milton.* Random House Publishing Group.
     Digital, 5967-5982 on Kindle.

times larger than the Waldensian population they were hunting, pursued the unfortunate believers into the higher reaches of the mountains. Desperate to find safety, the Waldenses loaded their elders and children into carts and began to climb the slopes of Mount Pelvoux, some 6,000 feet above the valley floor.

Halfway up the mountain, the desperate refugees found a little sliver of hope: a large cave. It was an ideal spot. There was a huge platform in front of the cave's mouth where the Waldensian men could stand watch and alert the rest of the group should they spot the pursuing army making their way up the mountainside. It was an easy spot to defend, so they quickly took shelter. The women, children, and elderly retreated inside the cave, and the entrance was barricaded with large stones.

What they didn't count on was the army ascending the mountain by a different route, and then suddenly descending to the mouth of the cave with ropes. The Waldensians were completely caught by surprise, and those posted outside as watchmen quickly retreated to the safety of the cave. The commander leading the troops watched them disappear into the dark, but he didn't want to follow them in because he believed that it would be far too dangerous to try and fight inside the cave. So he piled wood in front of the cave and lit it on fire. The inside filled with thick, black smoke, and the Waldensians were hopelessly trapped. They had two awful choices: they could run outside and die by the sword, or suffocate inside the cave. According to some sources, more than 3,000 died, including 400 babies who were later found in their mothers' arms. It was the death of an entire town.

Century after century, the Waldensians were hit over and over—but they did not die in vain. Their influence, like the early Celtic Christians, spread across the remnants of the Western Roman Empire, and in an age of suffocating darkness, countless thousands had an opportunity to hear the gospel. As mainstream Christianity shifted its focus to more Constantine-like concerns—money, power, and political influence—the woman hiding in the wilderness was shining a light in the darkness.

Jesus had made a promise that before His return, the gospel would be preached in all the world as a witness (Matthew 24:14), and nothing—absolutely nothing—would be permitted to stop it. As the pale horse made its ghastly way across the pages of history, the fifth seal was suddenly opened, and the voices of martyrs were heard crying out:

> *When He opened the fifth seal, I saw under the altar the souls of those who had been slain for the word of God and for the testimony which they held. And they cried with a loud voice, saying, "How long, O Lord, holy and true, until You judge and avenge our blood on those who dwell on the earth?"* (Revelation 6:9, 10)

Their cries had not gone unnoticed by heaven.

CHAPTER EIGHT:
HERE I STAND

"But hold fast what you have till I come. And he who overcomes, and keeps My works until the end, to him I will give power over the nations—'He shall rule them with a rod of iron; they shall be dashed to pieces like the potter's vessels'—as I also have received from My Father; and I will give him the morning star. He who has an ear, let him hear what the Spirit says to the churches." (Revelation 2:25-29)

THE CELTIC MISSIONARIES LEVIED AN UNDENIABLE impact on the remnants of the Roman Empire, carrying a biblical form of Christianity as far south as Italy. The Waldensians, who paid for their faith in blood, spread copies of the Scriptures all through the Western and Northern reaches. As the world headed into the 14th century, a priest and professor at Oxford by the name of John Wycliffe suddenly came under the conviction that the Scriptures ought to be available in the vernacular, or the language of the people. He took Jerome's Latin Vulgate and translated it into English in 1382.

Prophetically, it was the period of both the pale horse and the Church of Thyatira,[81] the time of tragic compromise between church and state that emerged after Constantine's legitimization of Christianity. Europe had just undergone the Black Death. "At the height of the Church's power," authors Larry Mansch and Curtis Peters explain, "and perhaps of its corruption, the Plague struck Europe in 1347. In just a dozen years nearly two hundred million people, somewhere between one-third and one-half of the population, perished. If the Black Death was not the end of the world, as many thought, then it surely was a sign of God's wrath."[82]

Those who lived through the plague viewed it as a judgment from God. To be sure, the timing fits the timeline of Revelation perfectly: any diligent student of Bible prophecy would have known that a catastrophe was bound to strike during the time of the Church of Thyatira:

> "And I gave her time to repent of her sexual immorality, and she did not repent. Indeed I will cast her into a sickbed, and those who commit adultery with her into great tribulation, unless they repent of their deeds. I will kill her children with death, and all the churches shall know that I am He who searches the minds and hearts. And I will give to each one of you according to your works." (Revelation 2:21-23)

---

81 See Chapter Four for a quick explanation of the seven churches.

82 Mansch, Larry D. and Peters, Curtis H. *Martin Luther: The Life and Lessons.* McFarland & Company, Inc. Digital, 299-301 on Kindle.

There was no darker time in the history of Western Christianity. The church became obsessed with political power, and those who wished to live by the simple principles of the gospel were persecuted. Living conditions in Europe were abysmal, particularly for those who lacked title or status. Millions died, either in the wake of the plague or by the sword of a church that did not permit liberty of conscience.

The church, after centuries of compromise, had become hopelessly corrupt:

Over the centuries the papacy had become obsessed with ceremony and form over substance. Popes lived beyond their means in divine opulence, constructed magnificent buildings, and patronized the arts. They financed wars and defended their territory, which included vast holdings of property throughout the continent. Accordingly, popes constantly needed cash, and they found a steady stream of revenue in Germany, the wealthiest country in Christendom. With no strong central government to protect them, German peasants had no alternative but to grumble and comply.

Popes collected their monies through bishops, who imposed taxes through their dioceses. Bishops established transactional taxes on contracts, mortgages, marriages, probates, and disputes in papal courts between clergy and parishioners. Rome even found a way to impose taxes on the new bishops the pope had just appointed. But these appointees who would now hold political and ecclesiastical power were seldom, if ever,

Germans, a fact that did not sit well with the increasingly nationalistic populace. In fact, the new appointees often didn't even travel to Germany, but sent vicars to fulfill their duties instead. These lower clergy, as they were called, were often poorly educated in both spiritual and non-spiritual matters. Worse, they behaved not as men of God, but as men of the world.

Bribery was rampant at all levels of the Church, and avarice was commonplace. Clerical concubinage was an open secret throughout the regions, and many parish priests held common law wives and children. Monastic compliance with their vows varied from order to order. (The Benedictines and Teutonic Knights seemed to have been most worldly, while the Dominican, Franciscan, and Augustinian friars were known to more strictly cling to their vows and perform regular acts of charity and benevolence.) For generations, even popes had been less than discreet with their own dalliances, and Pope Alexander, for one, had publicly acknowledged his own child. Historians agree that the condition of the Church as a whole, from top to bottom, gave great cause for alarm.[83]

This was the world in which Wycliffe was stirred to action. It is not by accident that he is known as the "Morning Star of the Reformation." In fulfillment of the promise that those who endured the depths of the Dark Ages would receive the "morning

83 Ibid., 299-301.

star" (Revelation 2:28), the lights were about to start coming on all over the European continent.

Wycliffe's English translation was only the beginning; his conviction that the Bible was the only reliable guide to truth, coupled with his preaching, had a powerful impact on those who heard him. One of his students, Jerome of Prague, was so inspired by what he heard from Wycliffe that he returned to Bohemia to share the gospel with anybody who would listen:

> *Among many on whose hearts such words fell with power was Jan Hus (John Huss), theological doctor and preacher in Prague, and confessor to the Queen of Bohemia. His sincere faith and striking abilities, with his eloquence and charm of manner, wrought mightily among people already prepared by the labours of the Waldenses who had been before him. . . . . The Pope, through the Archbishop of Prague, excommunicated Huss and had Wycliffe's writings publicly burned, but the king of Bohemia, the nobility, the University, and the majority of the people supported Huss and his teaching.*[84]

The Council of Constance, in 1415, declared Wycliffe a heretic and determined that his remains should not be permitted to remain buried in sanctified ground. A few years later, in 1428, his body was exhumed, the corpse was burned, and his ashes were scattered ignominiously in the River Swift. The Council also tried to persuade Huss to stop preaching his message of salvation by grace through faith, but their efforts were in vain.

---

84 Broadbent, Edmund. *The Pilgrim Church*. London: Pickering & Inglis, 1931, 145.

Huss responded by declaring that he would gladly recant any position that could be proven wrong by the Scriptures. The Council declared that Huss had been "infected with the leprosy of the Waldenses,"[85] and he was burned at the stake. Just days before his execution, Huss penned these incredible words:

> *O most Holy Christ, draw me, weak as I am, after Thyself, for if Thou dost not draw us we cannot follow Thee. Strengthen my spirit, that it may be willing. If the flesh is weak, let Thy grace prevent us; come between and follow, for without Thee we cannot go for Thy sake to a cruel death. Give me a fearless heart, a right faith, a firm hope, a perfect love, that for Thy sake I may lay down my life with patience and joy. Amen. Written in prison, in chains, on the eve of St. John the Baptist.*[86]

One after the other, more and more voices joined the swelling chorus that called for Christians to shed the centuries of compromise and superstition that had grabbed hold of the church, and to return to the primitive faith of the New Testament. The long ages of hardship endured by the faithful woman in the wilderness were about to bear fruit in a spectacular way.

On the November 10, 1483, Hans Luther, a miner by trade, and his wife, Margaretta, welcomed their first baby into the world. Few remember John and Margaret (as they're sometimes referred to), but everybody knows their son: Martin. In 1497, at the age of 14, Martin Luther was sent to Magdeburg to at-

---

85　Ibid., 146.

86　Ibid., 147.

tend a Franciscan school where discipline was so harsh that Luther mentions having been flogged 15 times in a single day. It echoed and amplified the harsh discipline meted out by his own father, and likely contributed to the tortured sense of guilt and self-loathing he later experienced as a monk. In addition to the severe punishments he received at the hands of his educators, his low station in life also meant that he had to beg for food by singing door to door.

In time, he found a benefactor in the town of Eisenach: Ursula Cotta, a woman who had heard him singing in the church choir and had seen the abuse heaped on him by some of her neighbors when he asked for food. Taking pity on the young scholar, she convinced her husband to take Luther into their home, after which he was able to stop begging for food.

At the age of 18, in compliance with his father's wishes, Luther began the study of law at the University of Erfurt. He quickly took to the classics, developing a fondness for the writers whose work had been endangered by the disrupting of the Western Roman Empire by his barbarian ancestors more than a thousand years earlier: Aristotle, Virgil, Cicero, and others. (Luther would later repudiate Aristotle, declaring that if the great philosopher had not been known to be a man, he would have taken him to be a devil.[87])

A lover of books, he spent long hours perusing the university library, and in his 20th year, he stumbled across a book that would not only change him, but the world through him: the Bible.

It was Jerome's Latin Vulgate, the version that Wycliffe had translated into English a century and a half earlier. Up to

---

87 D'Aubigné, J. H. Merle. *History of the Reformation of the Sixteenth Century*, Book I, Ch. III. Grand Rapids, MI: Baker Book House, 1987, 54.

this point, Luther had only heard brief snippets of the Bible read aloud in church, and he had no idea that there was more to the story:

> *The first page on which he fixes his attention narrates the story of Hannah and of the young Samuel. He reads— and his soul can hardly contain the joy it feels. This child, whom his parents led to the Lord as long as he liveth; the song of Hannah, in which she declares that Jehovah "raiseth up the poor out of the dust, and lifteth the beggar from the dunghill, to set them among princes;" this child, who grew up in the temple in the presence of the Lord; those sacrificers, the sons of Eli, who are wicked men, who live in debauchery, and "make the Lord's people to transgress;"—all this history, all this revelation that he has just discovered, excites feelings till then unknown. He returns home with a full heart. "Oh! that God would give me such a book for myself," thought he.*[88]

Of all the books that Luther had pulled off the shelf in his years at the university, this was the one that would launch a revolution. It was the same book that had inspired the early Celts, had galvanized the Waldensians to stand firm in the face of impossible odds, had whispered to Wycliffe that the common people needed access to it, and had steeled Huss to preach the gospel in spite of opposition that would lead to a pyre. It was the same book that had sparked revivals among the Israelites of old, when they read it aloud in repentance, and the book to which the risen Jesus Himself directed His disillusioned followers when their

---

88   Ibid.

faith was shattered in the wake of the crucifixion. "And beginning at Moses and all the Prophets, He expounded to them in all the Scriptures the things concerning Himself." (Luke 24:27)

There is a reason the Bible stirs hearts unlike any other book: it is the revelation of Christ Himself, from Genesis to Revelation. It does not change hearts merely through persuasive argument or historical fact, although both can be found in its pages. It changes hearts because it is "God-breathed,"[89] and is the voice of the Creator to our world.

The moment had come when the first sparks of the Reformation were to be fanned into an unstoppable flame. Luther's transformation was not instantaneous, but those quiet moments in the library started him down a difficult path to an epiphany that would change everything.

Luther became so devoted to study that he neglected his health, and it deteriorated so rapidly that it appeared as if he would soon die. As he laid on his deathbed, an old priest came to visit him. "Soon," Luther told the clergyman, "I shall be called away from this world."[90] The priest, who had been watching Luther's academic career with interest, challenged Luther's pessimistic assumption. "Take heart," he told the young Reformer-to-be, "You shall not die of this sickness; God will make you one who will comfort many others; on those whom he loves he lays the holy cross, and they who bear it patiently learn wisdom."[91]

---

89 "All Scripture is given by inspiration of God." (2 Timothy 3:16). The original Greek word for "inspiration" is *theopneustos,* which literally means that God "breathed out" the Scriptures.

90 D'Aubigné, 55.

91 Wylie, J.A. *The History of Protestantism.* Harrington, DE: Delmarva Publications, 2013. Digital, 7484-7485 on Kindle.

Luther took the priest's words as a promise from God that he would survive, and he recovered. His friend, Alexis, however, was not so lucky: in the prime of life, he was struck down by an assassin. The news left Luther reeling; how could such a thing happen to his friend? "And what," he wondered to himself, "would become of *me* if *I* were murdered?"[92] He found himself tortured by the uncertainty of death and the hereafter.

In the summer of 1505, Luther had another occasion to consider his mortality and eternal destiny. After returning home to visit his parents, he found himself suddenly caught up in a violent thunderstorm on his way back to Erfurt. He was nearing the village of Stotternheim when a bolt of lightning struck the ground so close to his feet that it knocked him over. Terrified, the young scholar yelped out a prayer to St. Anne, the patron saint of miners: "St. Anne! Help me, and I will become a monk."

His fate was sealed. His father had wanted him to be a man of power and influence—a lawyer—but his life had been miraculously spared, and he yielded to the growing conviction he had harbored for some time: that he should enter the ministry. On August 17, 1505, Luther threw a small party for his friends, and when dinner was finished, he left his home, walked straight to the Augustinian Convent, knocked on the door, and to the sharp disappointment of his father, entered the monastic life.

Luther's brushes with mortality caused him a great deal of anxiety, and life in the cloister did not bring him the peace of mind he'd hoped for. In the beginning, during his first year as a novice, he was enthusiastic about his new life. His rigid upbringing and disciplinarian educational experience prepared him for the demanding schedule of monastic life. Prayers were

---

92   D'Aubigné, 55.

scheduled seven times a day, the first coming in the wee hours of the morning, between 1- 2 a.m. A year later, Luther was convinced he was on the right path and took his vows.

He was not to enjoy the quiet life of a monk for long, however. His superior decided that Luther had been called to the priesthood. His father—apparently somewhat reconciled to Luther's new life—accepted an invitation to be present as the new priest said his first mass on May 2, 1507.

It was understood that a priest had the power and authority to transform the elements of communion—the bread and the wine—into the literal body and blood of Christ. As Luther prepared to perform the rite, he was suddenly struck by the words he had begun to recite: "We offer unto thee, the living, the true, the eternal God." In Luther's own words:

> *At these words I was utterly stupefied and terror-stricken. I thought to myself, "With what tongue shall I address such Majesty, seeing that all men ought to tremble in the presence of even an earthly prince? Who am I, that I should lift up mine eyes to the divine Majesty? The angels surround him. At his nod the earth trembles. And shall I, a miserable little pygmy, say, "I want this, I ask for that?" For I am dust and ashes and full of sin and I am speaking to the living, eternal and the true God.*[93]

Luther became paralyzed with fear, spilling a little wine and nearly dropping the bread. He turned to the prior who had been assisting him and mentioned that he wanted to stop reciting the

---

93 Bainton, Roland. *Here I Stand: A Life of Martin Luther*. Nashville: Abingdon Press, 1950, 41.

mass and leave. The irritated prior urged him to get on with the business at hand, and Luther struggled his way through the rest of the rite.

Afterward, there was a celebratory meal, at which Luther sat down with his father. It bothered him that Hans did not approve of his choice to pursue a religious vocation, and he cautiously asked his father why he had objected. Hans' anger and frustration with his son came to a head. "You learned scholar," he boiled over, "have you never read in the Bible that you should honor your father and your mother? And here you have left me and your mother to look after ourselves in our old age."[94]

Luther responded that he could do his father much more good by praying for him in the church than by living a worldly life. And besides, he pointed out, God had clearly called him in the thunderstorm near Stotternheim. "God grant," his father answered, "that it was not an apparition of the Devil."[95]

So began the religious career of the most notorious priest in history. And while he clearly yearned for his father's approval, his bigger struggle was finding acceptance with his Heavenly Father. Having grown up steeped more in God's judgment than mercy, he struggled with becoming good enough. His days as a monk were filled with strict discipline, privation, and self-imposed punishments, in an attempt to reconcile his sinful life and guilty conscience with the notion of a perfect and holy God. But no matter how often he starved himself, denied himself the comforts of life, or whipped himself, he continued to find no satisfaction that he had been accepted of God.

In later years, Luther would state to Duke George of Saxony:

94 Ibid, 42.

95 Ibid.

It is true, I was a pious monk, and so strictly did I observe the rules of my order that I may say: If ever a monk got to heaven through monasticism I, too, would have got there. To this all my associates in the cloister, who knew me, will bear witness. If this life had lasted longer, I would have martyred myself to death with the vigils, praying, reading, and other labor.[96]

Even the slightest slip-up would plunge Luther into deep despair:

I tortured myself almost to death in order to procure peace with God for my troubled heart and agitated conscience; but surrounded with thick darkness, I found peace nowhere.[97]

While I was yet a monk, I no sooner felt assailed by any temptation than I cried out—I am lost! Immediately I had recourse to a thousand methods to stifle the cries of my conscience. I went every day to confession, but that was of no use to me. Then bowed down by sorrow, I tortured myself by the multitude of my thoughts.—Look, exclaimed I, thou art still envious, impatient, passionate! . . . It profiteth thee nothing, O wretched man, to have entered this sacred order.[98]

---

96 Mansch, Larry D. and Curtis H. Peters. *Martin Luther: The Life and Lessons.* McFarland & Company, Inc. Digital, 5096-5099 on Kindle.

97 D'Aubigné, 60.

98 Ibid.

Luther took to the confessional like a starving man takes to bread; he couldn't get enough. His confessors soon realized that he was a tortured soul who would launch into impossibly detailed descriptions of even the most minor transgressions, such as spilling his food or arriving late for choir. His confessions could last for hours at a time, and even when he was finished, he would sometimes think of additional sins on his way out and return to confess them.

It was in the depths of despair that he met Johann Staupitz, the vicar general of the Augustinian order at the University of Wittenberg. After listening to Luther's struggle to find forgiveness, and enduring a confession that lasted six hours, he took pity on the monk, whom he considered to have great potential. Staupitz attempted to give Luther some peace of mind. "Why do you torture yourself with these thoughts?" he asked him. "Look at the wounds of Christ. Look at the blood Christ shed for you. It is there the grace of God will appear to you."

Luther pushed back. "I cannot and I dare not come to God till I am a better man," he protested.

"A better man!" Staupitz replied. "Christ came to save not good men, but sinners. Love God, and you will have repented; there is no real repentance that does not begin in the love of God; and there is no love to God that does not take its rise in all apprehension of that mercy which offers to sinners freedom from sin through the blood of Christ."[99]

---

99 In Wylie's *History of Protestantism*, 7647-7651 on Kindle. Wylie's use of the phrase "would the Vicar-General say in effect" suggests that perhaps this is not a direct quote, but rather the author's effort to summarize Staupitz' thoughts.

Staupitz gave Luther a Bible before he left Erfurt, and it was the beginning of Luther's journey to spiritual healing. The first shards of doubt were beginning to pierce his obsession with finding forgiveness and righteousness through his own efforts. Shortly after the encounter, he once again fell ill, and a fellow monk paid him a visit. He recited the Apostles' Creed in Luther's hearing, and asked the ailing man to repeat after him. "I believe in the forgiveness of sins," Luther echoed the monk.

"No," the monk said. "You are to believe not merely in the forgiveness of David's sins, and of Peter's sins; you must believe in the forgiveness of your own sins."[100]

It was at that moment that the counsel Staupitz had given him took root. He suddenly realized that he had been trying to win God's favor, when God had loved him all along. His sins were not to be forgiven after he had impressed God, because "while we were still sinners, Christ died for us." (Romans 5:8) God's forgiveness is not earned, it is *given*. Freely.

"We love Him because He first loved us." (1 John 4:19)

"If it had not been for Dr. Staupitz," Luther said, "I should have sunk in hell."[101]

In 1510, at the age of 27, Luther was sent to Rome as a delegate to a council called to settle a dispute that had erupted among a number of Augustinian monasteries—a testament to his diligence as a monk and the confidence his superiors placed in him. Naturally, he was thrilled at the prospect of visiting the Eternal City, the center of the world as far as the church was concerned. What he discovered in Rome, however,

---

100 Ibid.

101 Bainton, 53.

left him disillusioned. As he crossed the mountains into Italy, he noticed that the monasteries were not simple or austere like the ones he knew at home. The monks who lived closer to Rome were living like princes, in well-appointed luxury, and they disregarded most of the rules of the monastic order in order to live a life of leisure.

Rome was little better. When the papacy had moved to France in 1309, the city of Rome was neglected and fell into a state of shocking disrepair. In time, trash and debris littered the streets, wild animals roamed freely, and the countryside surrounding the city became a haven for criminals. The original St. Peter's Basilica, built by Constantine on the spot where Peter is believed to have been crucified, fell into disrepair.

If the city itself had become decrepit, then the morals of the clergy were in even worse shape. Luther had expected the monks and priests of the Mother City to live as he did, in spartan monastic cells on a peasant's diet. What he found was a degree of self-indulgence and wanton hedonism that made his encounters with the monks of northern Italy seem tame by comparison. The local priests laughed at his simple piety, suggesting that as a German, he did not possess the sophistication they had employed to skirt the system and benefit from it. The Roman clergy considered Luther a dull relic of an austere past.

On one occasion, as Luther was saying mass, local priests started to mock him for his deliberate, careful pacing. It was said that in the time it took Luther to say a single mass, the locals were able to recite seven! Worse, Luther soon discovered that many of his fellow clergy did not even believe in what they were doing. Some had substituted the words *hoc est meum corpus*

("This is My body") with the words *panis es, et panis manebis*: "Bread thou art, and bread thou wilt remain."[102]

It was devastating to Luther's confidence:

> *Instead of a city of prayers and alms, of contrite hearts and holy lives, Rome was full of mocking hypocrisy, defiant skepticism, jeering impiety, and shameless revelry. Borgia had lately closed his infamous Pontificate, and the warlike Julius II was now reigning. A powerful police patrolled the city every night. They were empowered to deal summary justice on offenders, and those whom they caught were hanged at the next post or thrown into the Tiber. But all the vigilance of the patrol could not secure the peace and safety of the streets. Robberies and murders were of nightly occurrence. "If there be a hell,"* said Luther, *"Rome is built over it."*[103]

The dejected Luther decided to visit the *Scala Sancta*, or the Holy Stairs, in order to pray. The stairs, located next to the Lateran Palace, were said to be the very steps on which Jesus left the judgment hall of Pilate on the night of His trial. It was rumored that the stairs, had been brought to Rome by Constantine's mother, Helena, in the 4th century.[104] Pilgrims, as they still do today, would ascend the steps on their knees in an act of penance, which is precisely what Luther was hoping to do. Partway up the steps, however, a passage from Paul's letter to the Romans

---

102 Wylie, *History of Protestantism*, 7973-7974.

103 Ibid., 7979-7983.

104 There are some old accounts in print that suggested the stairs had been transported to Rome by angels.

suddenly flashed into his mind so powerfully that it was as if a voice had spoken from heaven: "The just shall live by faith." (Romans 1:17)

It was not the first time Paul's statement—a quote from the Old Testament book of Habakkuk—had electrified his mind. On two previous occasions, the same verse had suddenly inspired Luther in a moment of darkness. This was, however, the decisive moment that changed everything. Suddenly relieved of the need to try and earn his salvation, he rose to his feet and left.

He returned to Germany in February 1511, where in due course, Luther was made a professor at the University of Wittenberg. Recognizing Luther's potential, Staupitz decided that Luther should also become the Chair of Bible at the university, which meant he would have to start preaching publicly. If Luther was required to teach the Bible to others, Staupitz reasoned, he would also have to pay careful attention to its content for himself. It might just be the thing that solidified Luther's newfound commitment to the doctrine of grace.

One day, under a pear tree where Luther was known to sit, the Vicar-General presented the idea. Luther didn't like the thought of becoming a public preacher, and protested strenuously. His protests fell on deaf ears, however; Staupitz' mind had been made up. Luther had little choice but to become an expert in the Scriptures. In 1513, he began a lecture series on the book of Psalms. In 1515, he started in on the book of Romans, followed by a series on the book of Galatians . . . which carried him into the fateful year 1517.

By that time, the tortuous experiences Luther had passed through, coupled with a concentrated study of God's Word, led him to become completely disillusioned with an ecclesiastical structure that had obviously become corrupt. He had not yet become Luther the Reformer, but all that changed when a fund-raising campaign for a brand-new basilica in Rome pushed him over the edge.

Pope Julius II, who had named himself not for the original Pontiff by that name, but for Julius Caesar, had visions of creating the greatest monument to Christianity in the world. Recognizing that the original St. Peter's was in a state of decay, he decided to knock most of it down and replace it with a much grander structure, one that would become the greatest building in Christendom and the second-largest church in the world.

Previous efforts at restoration and expansion had taken place under Pope Nicholas V in the 15th century, but it was Julius II who truly got the project rolling. The new basilica, he reasoned, would also be a perfect home for the massive white marble tomb he had commissioned Michelangelo to create for him. (The tomb of Julius II was never actually installed in the new St. Peter's; the scale of the original design was reduced considerably, and it now resides at the Church of St. Pietro in Vincoli. The famous "horned Moses" statue is a part of the tomb.)[105]

When Julius II died, Leo X inherited the building project. Leo was the head of the Medici family—bankers to kings and Popes—and knew how to spend money. Before long, the funds

---

105 It is widely believed that Julius II found the original St Peter's an insufficient home for his future tomb, and that his desire to rebuild was driven by pride and a desire to be properly displayed posthumously in a more grandiose setting. While it does seem to match the character of the man, it should be noted that some historians have disputed this, suggesting that nothing specific can be found in the historical record to confirm the suspicion. There is little doubt that had his original plans succeeded, his memory would have indeed loomed large in the new basilica.

earmarked for the new basilica had been spent, and Leo needed to find a new source of money.

Recognizing the potential that religion has for creating wealth, on March 15, 1517, he offered an indulgence to everyone who contributed to the building fund. An indulgence was a reduction (or even remittance) of time spent in purgatory, and could be obtained for yourself or for your dead relatives who were said to be suffering there. Across Europe, monarchs grumbled that Rome had thought of yet another way to drain their coffers, until it was arranged in various countries that the heads of state could receive a percentage of what was raised. In Germany, Albrecht of Brandenburg, the Archbishop of Mainz, had borrowed 20,000 florins to pay Rome for his nomination to the post. His creditors, worried he might never pay them back, arranged to receive a cut of each indulgence sold in order to recoup their loan.

Albrecht's chief indulgence salesman was Johann Tetzel, a Dominican friar who had once served as the grand inquisitor in Poland. In 1517, as Luther was busy finishing his sermon series on Galatians, Tetzel was assigned to sell indulgences in the dioceses of Magdeburg and Halberstadt:

> As he approached a town, he was met by the dignitaries, who then entered with him in solemn procession. A cross bearing the papal arms preceded him, and the pope's bull of indulgence was borne aloft on gold-embroidered velvet cushion. The cross was solemnly planted in the market place, and the sermon began.

> Listen now, God and St. Peter call you. Consider the salvation of your souls and those of your loved ones

departed. You priest, you noble, you merchant, you virgin, you matron, you youth, you old man, enter now into your church, which is the Church of St. Peter. Visit the most holy cross erected before you and ever imploring you. Have you considered that you are lashed in a furious tempest amid the temptations and dangers of the world, and that you do not know whether you can reach the haven, not of your mortal body, but of your immortal soul? Consider that all who are contrite and have confessed and made contribution will receive complete remission of all their sins. Listen to the voices of your dear dead relatives and friends, beseeching you and saying, "Pity us, pity us. We are in dire torment from which you can redeem us for a pittance." Do you not wish to? Open your ears. Hear the father saying to his son, the mother to her daughter, "We bore you, nourished you, brought you up, left you our fortunes, and you are so cruel and hard that now you are not willing for so little to set us free. Will you let us lie here in flames? will you delay our promised glory? Remember that you are able to release them, for

As soon as the coin in the coffer rings,
The soul from purgatory springs.

Will you not then for a quarter of a florin receive these letters of indulgence through which you are able to lead a divine and immortal soul into the fatherland of paradise? [106]

---

106 Bainton, 77-78.

Tetzel may have been preaching in a neighboring community, but enough of Martin Luther's parishioners were slipping over to hear Tetzel speak that he became painfully aware of what was going on. When Luther told sinners that the only effective way to find forgiveness was to repent, some of them produced a letter of indulgence from Tetzel, declaring that the matter had already been settled. Luther was outraged—after having struggled for so long to accept the loving character of God, the thought of selling forgiveness angered him.

Word of Luther's refusal to endorse the indulgences reached Tetzel, and he publicly denounced Luther. In return, Luther penned 95 theological propositions for debate, now known as his famous "95 Theses." At noon on October 31, 1517, on the eve of All Saints' Day, when the sacred relics of Frederick the Elector would be on display and attract large crowds, Luther nailed his document to the door of the Castle Church in Wittenberg.

It was not an act of vandalism; propositions for discussion or debate were commonly posted on the church door. The title of Luther's document? "Disputation for Clarification of the Power of Indulgences."

The fallout from that document? While Luther never meant for his theses to be published across Christendom (although he did provide a German copy for the general public to read), he did send a copy to Albrecht of Mainz, along with a letter:

> *God on high, is this the way the souls entrusted to your care are prepared for death? It is high time that you looked into this matter. I can be silent no longer. In fear and trembling we must work out our salvation. Indulgences can offer no security but only the remission of external canonical*

penalties. Works of piety and charity are infinitely better than indulgences. Christ did not command the preaching of indulgences but of the gospel, and what a horror it is, what a peril to a bishop, if he never gives the gospel to his people except along with the racket of indulgences. In the instructions of Your Paternity to the indulgence sellers, issued without your knowledge and consent, indulgences are called the inestimable gift of God for the reconciliation of man to God and the emptying of purgatory. Contrition is declared to be unnecessary. What shall I do, Illustrious Prince, if not to beseech Your Paternity through Jesus Christ our Lord to suppress utterly these instructions lest someone arise to confute this book and to bring Your Illustrious Sublimity into obloquy, which I dread but fear if something is not done speedily? May Your Paternity accept my faithful admonition. I, too, am one of your sheep. May the Lord Jesus guard you forever. Amen.[107]

Luther's letter was forwarded to Leo X, who responded by suggesting that Luther had been drunk when he wrote it, and would feel better once he sobered up. Luther had no need to sober up, and neither did he forget about the matter. The German public, long fed up with the abuses of the church, thought of Luther as a sort of folk hero, the man who could take on a corrupt establishment. The revenues from the sale of indulgences began to plummet. In December, Tetzel published a reply—"106 Anti-Theses"— and in Wittenberg, a mob of university students assailed the man selling it and burned 800 copies in the town square.

107 Bainton, 84-85.

Luther replied to Tetzel from the pulpit. "If I am called heretic by those whose purses will suffer from my truths," he retorted, "I care not for their bawling; for only those say this whose dark understanding has never known the Bible."[108]

In March 1518, the vice-chancellor of the University of Ingolstadt, Johann Eck, who became famous for his disputes with the great Reformer, published a pamphlet against Luther's positions. In it, he identified Luther's positions as those of John Huss. (In that vein, Luther had also adopted, as had Huss, a number of Waldensian positions.)

In July, Leo X summoned Luther to appear in Rome. Luther appealed to Frederick, suggesting that Rome should not be able to extradite Germans, and the elector agreed. The German princes started to view Luther as a bargaining chip in their political and financial disputes with the papacy, which afforded Luther the kind of protection that John Huss did not enjoy. Leo then asked Luther to appear at the Diet of Augsburg (October 1518), in German territory. In the background, he started to flatter Frederick, presenting him with a much-coveted "Golden Rose" award, and suggesting that he might be next in line for Holy Roman Emperor should he render good service to the church.

At the Diet, Cardinal Cajetan demanded that Luther recant, and Luther refused. The debate raged for the next few years—Luther at various times assuming a submissive tone and then re-igniting his wrath against the hierarchy. Finally, on June 15, 1520, Leo issued his now-infamous bull, *Exsurge Domine,* which condemned a large number of statements made by Luther. If he did not recant within 60 days, the Pope said, Luther would be

---

108 Pastor, Ludwig. *History of the Popes.* In Will Durant, *The Reformation.* New York: Simon and Shuster, 1954, 346.

excommunicated. Luther's books were burned, first in Rome, and then in Cologne.

The bull reached Luther in October. He responded with a burning of his own at the gates of the university. In addition to a number of scholastic books, he burned a copy of *Exsurge Domine*.

Perhaps the most famous chapter in Luther's life was his appearance at the Diet of Worms in 1521. Called on once more to recant, Luther replied as only Luther could:

"Since then Your Majesty and your lordships desire a simple reply, I will answer without horns and without teeth. Unless I am convicted by Scripture and plain reason—I do not accept the authority of popes and councils, for they have contradicted each other—my conscience is captive to the Word of God. I cannot and I will not recant anything, for to go against conscience is neither right nor safe. God help me. Amen.[109] Here I stand, I cannot do otherwise."[110]

---

109 The next phrase—*Here I stand, I cannot do otherwise*—does not appear in every account of the speech, but does appear in the earliest printed account.

110 Bainton, 185.

EPILOGUE

*After these things I saw another angel coming down
from heaven, having great authority, and the earth was
illuminated with his glory.* (Revelation 18:1)

MOST PEOPLE KNOW THE NAME OF MARTIN LUTHER,
even though many in the 21st century understand little of what
he believed or accomplished. Over the course of half a millennium, much of what Luther fought for has faded into the background in a world where much of Christendom seems little
occupied with doctrinal matters. Some will acknowledge that
Luther taught both *Sola Scriptura* (the Bible alone as the supreme authority in doctrinal matters) and *Sola Fide* (salvation
by grace through faith alone). Beyond that, little else is known.

Even less is known about the fact that Luther was hardly
alone. Of course, there were other, earlier Reformers—Huss,
Wycliffe, and Tyndale, for example—but Luther was also standing on the shoulders of a thousand years of Christians who
chose to live a simple, biblical Christianity.

Luther's doctrinal positions—the sole authority of Scripture
as the supreme rule of faith, salvation by faith in the merits of
Christ alone, and even a clear understanding that the ecclesiastical
structure of the Middle Ages was the "falling away" predicted by
Bible prophecy—were not novel. He did not invent a new Chris-

tianity, but brought to light centuries-old traditions that had been hidden away on the fringes of the empire. The flames of the gospel had been miraculously kept alive by remote and unlikely groups like the early Celts and the Waldenses. There were others, equally remarkable, also living outside either the boundaries or control of Rome, but space does not permit a retelling of their stories.

The four horsemen of the Apocalypse have already come and gone: the white horse of the early apostolic church, the red horse of brave Christians persecuted by the pagan Romans, the black horse of church-state compromise after Constantine, and the pale horse, the church of the Dark Ages. For many long centuries, biblical Christianity was pushed to the very fringes of the known world—a woman hiding in the wilderness from the wrath of the dragon.

As the fifth seal was opened, voices cried for vindication:

> "How long, O Lord, holy and true, until You judge and avenge our blood on those who dwell on the earth?" (Revelation 6:10)

It was the cry of a people longing for the end of darkness—resolute in their faith, and determined to "not love their lives to the death." (Revelation 12:11)

Over time, changes came over many of the movements that labored in the darkness. At the Synod of Whitby in AD 664, an irreversible blow was dealt to the uniqueness of the Celtic church. The mainstream church had been making large advances in Britannia, especially after the arrival of Augustine of Canterbury, who was sent to Britain in AD 597 by Pope Gregory the Great. When Augustine's church came in contact with the Celt-

ic believers, they discovered that they differed on a number of
doctrinal issues, and conflict ensued. The king of Northumbria
was faced with a choice: would he side with the church of Rome,
or with the Celts?

The key issue on the table seems trivial, but sometimes
kingdoms rise and fall on seemingly trivial issues. The synod
was to determine the correct date for celebrating Easter. The
Celts, who observed a different date, were considered heretics. It
is noteworthy that such seemingly trivial matters could become
hot-button issues, when in the past it had taken much more sub-
stantive issues, such as challenging the divinity of Christ, to earn
the badge of "heretic." But those intent on building empires will
usually seek conformity at every level. (Demanding a unified
date for the remembrance of the resurrection of Christ is but the
tip of the iceberg when it comes to the coercive uniformity that
was demanded by the official state church; those who chose to
continue the observance of the seventh-day Sabbath were also
branded anathema.) Thomas Cahill commented:

> As it happened, the Irish party gave in—with a few hold-
> outs who came over in time. They agreed, however reluc-
> tantly, that their father in God, Columcille, whose name
> was involved in all their customs, took second place to
> Peter, the prince of the Lord's apostles, in whose name the
> Roman party made its argument. The solution, like the
> problem, was a simpleminded one: our relics—the bones
> of our founder—are holier than yours, so Rome is greater
> than Iona, and thus we've got right on our side.[111]

---

111 Cahill, 201.

The key to helping the Celts capitulate, it appears, was the influence of an Irish abbot named Cummian:

> *What thing more perverse [said he] can be felt of our church than if we say, "Rome is wrong, Jerusalem is wrong, Antioch is wrong, the whole world is wrong: only the Irish and the Britons know what is right, these peoples who are almost at the ends of the earth, and, you might say, a pimple on the chin of the world."* [112]

To the eye of empire-builders intent on consolidation, the Celts may have seemed like a "pimple on the chin of the world," but to the prophetic eye of Scripture, they were anything but. The king of Northumbria, faced with a choice between Rome and Iona, chose the former, after being informed that Peter held the keys to the kingdom and the wrong decision would mean being locked out of heaven.

Celtic missionary fervor continued for some time, as evidenced by their continued impact on the European continent and the long string of monasteries that continued to be built. But over the course of the next centuries—up to the invasion of England by the Vikings—the compromise of Whitby took its toll: the primitive Celtic church was gradually subsumed into the church of Constantine.

When news of Luther's Reformation spilled over the Alps and reached the Waldensian valleys, the Waldenses received the news with joy: they were no longer alone in their convictions. They immediately started dialogues with the Protestants, and eventually

---

112 Ibid., 202.

merged with the Calvinist tradition. The Waldenses are still with us to this day. They have a church just a stone's throw from St. Peter's, a marvelous hotel nearby, and worldwide, they boast nearly 50,000 members, most of whom live in South America.

In June 2015, Pope Francis visited the Waldensian church in Turin to ask for forgiveness. Prior to the Pope's speech, Eugenio Bernardini, the pastor, asked a powerful question: "What was the sin of the Waldensians? It was being a movement of popular evangelization, carried out by lay people."[113]

There was, in other words, no sin committed by their godly ancestors. Francis admitted as much and asked forgiveness for the "inhuman behavior" leveled against them, while being careful not to suggest that there were no lingering doctrinal differences.

As for the 500th anniversary of Luther's Theses, the Vatican has issued a postage stamp in his honor, which took many people by surprise, since he is still considered a divisive influence. In an attempt to further ecumenical discussions, Pope Francis made a trip to Sweden in the fall of 2016 in order to join a celebration of the Reformation's 500th birthday and dedicate a new statue of Luther—a move that upset a number of Vatican hard-liners. His declared intent was to find a way to readmit Lutherans to the Catholic communion.

As we consider the long conflict between compromise and biblical fidelity that played out over the course of the Dark Ages, careful students of Bible prophecy should note a couple of things:

---

113 www.catholicherald.co.uk/news/2015/06/22/pope-francis-asks-waldensi
     an-christians-to-forgive-the-church

1. Bible prophecy has been stunningly accurate over the span of more than 2,600 years. The predictions of Daniel, from the rise and fall of Babylon to the appearance of the little horn, have come to pass with breathtaking precision. We should expect that the rest of the Bible's predictions, which include a last-day revival of the beast of Revelation 13, will also undoubtedly transpire.

2. As the fiery passion of successive "church in the wilderness" movements waned, God always raised up another wave of brave voices to carry forward the propagation of the gospel. The Bible predicts that in the final moments of earth's history, there will be a "remnant" of the woman who once again take up the mantle and fearlessly proclaim God's truth. The experience of the Dark Ages, tragically, will be repeated.

Revelation 13 makes it plain that coercive religion will once again darken the earth—and while that transpires, a faithful group lights the world with God's final message to a fallen race:

> Then I looked, and behold, a Lamb standing on Mount Zion, and with Him one hundred and forty-four thousand, having His Father's name written on their foreheads. And I heard a voice from heaven, like the voice of many waters, and like the voice of loud thunder. And I heard the sound of harpists playing their harps. They sang as it were a new song before the throne, before the four living creatures, and the elders; and no one could learn that song except the hundred and forty-four thou-

sand who were redeemed from the earth. These are the ones who were not defiled with women, for they are virgins. These are the ones who follow the Lamb wherever He goes. These were redeemed from among men, being firstfruits to God and to the Lamb. And in their mouth was found no deceit, for they are without fault before the throne of God. Then I saw another angel flying in the midst of heaven, having the everlasting gospel to preach to those who dwell on the earth—to every nation, tribe, tongue, and people—saying with a loud voice, "Fear God and give glory to Him, for the hour of His judgment has come; and worship Him who made heaven and earth, the sea and springs of water." And another angel followed, saying, "Babylon is fallen, is fallen, that great city, because she has made all nations drink of the wine of the wrath of her fornication." Then a third angel followed them, saying with a loud voice, "If anyone worships the beast and his image, and receives his mark on his forehead or on his hand, he himself shall also drink of the wine of the wrath of God, which is poured out full strength into the cup of His indignation. He shall be tormented with fire and brimstone in the presence of the holy angels and in the presence of the Lamb. And the smoke of their torment ascends forever and ever; and they have no rest day or night, who worship the beast and his image, and whoever receives the mark of his name." Here is the patience of the saints; here are those who keep the commandments of God and the faith of Jesus. (Revelation 14:1-12)

Many a Christian has looked back on the stories of brave martyrs in quiet admiration. "Given a chance," some whisper to themselves, "I would have stood for truth, too. I wish I had lived when Christianity *meant* something."

You will still get your chance. Bible prophecy divides the last generation into only two camps: those willing to compromise, and those who "follow the Lamb wherever He goes." The faithful remnant persists until the return of Christ, and triumphs through the last great crisis.

Given the content of the final message to this fallen planet—the message of three angels—it is clear that there will be a body of believers, those who "keep the commandments of God and the faith of Jesus," who continue traveling the path blazed by the Celts, the Waldenses, the Reformers, and others.

Ask yourself: what did so many people see in the Scriptures that made them so utterly unafraid in the darkest of hours? Why were their lives marked by such fearless passion? What did they find that they considered more valuable than life itself?

Perhaps now, before the next crisis breaks, is the time to find out.

BIBLIOGRAPHY

Andrews, John Nevin. *History of the Sabbath*. Payson, AZ: Leaves of Autumn, 1998.

Augustine of Hippo. *The City of God*. New York: Modern Library Edition, 1993.

Bainton, Roland. *Here I Stand: A Life of Martin Luther*. Nashville: Abingdon Press, 1950.

Barbero, Alessandro. *The Day of the Barbarians: The Epic Battle that Began the Fall of the Roman Empire*. London: Atlantic Books, 2007.

Beattie, William. *The Waldenses*. London: George Virtue, 1838.

Boonstra, Shawn. *Shadow Emperor*. Loveland, CO: Voice of Prophecy, 2016.

Broadbent, Edmund. *The Pilgrim Church*. London: Pickering & Inglis, 1931.

Cahill, Thomas. *How the Irish Saved Civilization*. New York: Doubleday, 1996.

D'Aubigné, J. H. Merle. *History of the Reformation of the Sixteenth Century*. Grand Rapids, MI: Baker Book House, 1987.

Durant, Will. *The Reformation, a History of European Civilization From Wycliff to Calvin: 1300-1564*. New York: Simon and Schuster, 1957.

Edwards, Jonathan. *The History of the Work of Redemption*. Worcester, MA: Isaiah Thomas and Leonard Worcester, 1792.

Fletcher, Richard. *The Barbarian Conversion: From Paganism to Christianity*. Los Angeles: University of California Press, 1999.

Green, Michael. *Evangelism in the Early Church*. Guildford, Surrey: Hodder and Stoughton, 1970.

Hardinge, Leslie. *The Celtic Church in Britain*. Brushton, New York: Teach Services, 1995.

Heather, Peter. *Empires and Barbarians*. New York: Oxford University Press, 2009.

Herm, Gerhard. *The Celts: The People Who Came out of Darkness*. New York: Barnes and Noble, 1993.

Kerrigan, William, et al. *The Complete Poetry and Essential Prose of John Milton*. New York: Random House, 2007.

Knecht, R. J. *Francis I*. New York: Cambridge University Press, 1982.

Kousoulas, D. G. *The Life and Times of Constantine the Great*. NP: BookSurge Publishing, 2007.

LaHaye, Tim and Jerry B. Jenkins. *Are We Living in the End Times?* Wheaton: Tyndale House, 1999.

Lindsey, Hal. *The Late Great Planet Earth*. Zondervan, Kindle Edition.

Miller, Keith. *St. Peter's*. London: Profile Books, 2009.

Minchin-Comm, Dorothy and Hyveth B. Williams. *The Celt and the Christ: Another Look at the Letter to the Galatians*. Victoria, BC: Trafford Publishing, 2008.

Moffat, Alistair. *The Sea Kingdoms: The History of Celtic Britain and Ireland*. London: HarperCollins, 2001.

Monastier, Antoine. *A History of the Vaudois Church from its Origin and of the Vaudois of Piedmont to the Present Day*. London: Religious Tract Society, 1848.

Muston, Alexis. *The Waldenses: Sketches of the Evangelical Christians of the Valleys of Piedmont*. Philadelphia: Presbyterian Board of Publication, 1853.

Neander, Augustus. *General History of the Christian Religion and Church*. Translation by Joseph Torrey. London: Henry G. Bohn, 1852.

Robb, Graham. *The Discovery of Middle Earth: Mapping the Lost World of the Celts*. New York: W. W. Norton & Co., 2013.

Robinson, Robert. *Ecclesiastical Researches*. Cambridge: Francis Hodson, 1792.

Scotti, R. A. *Basilica, The Splendor and the Scandal: Building St Peter's*. New York: Plume Printing, 2007.

Staunton, Michael. *The Voice of the Irish: The Story of Christian Ireland*. Mahweh, New Jersey: HiddenSpring, 2003.

Stephenson, Paul. *Constantine: Roman Emperor, Christian Victor*. Overlook Press, 2010.

Strand, Kenneth, ed. *The Sabbath in Scripture and History*. Washington, DC: Review and Herald, 1982.

Waddington, George. *History of the Church, From the Earliest Ages to the Reformation (Classic Reprint)*. Kindle Edition.

Wilkinson, Benjamin G. *Truth Triumphant*. Portland, OR: Pacific Press, 1944.

Wilson, Derek. *Charlemagne*. New York, Vintage Books, 2005.

Wylie, James A. *The History of Protestantism*. Harrington, DE: Delmarva Publications, 2013.

Wylie, James A. *The History of the Waldenses*. Harrington, DE: Delmarva Publications, 2013.

Xavier, Neil O'Donaghue, trans. *St. Patrick: His Confession and Other Works*. New Jersey: Catholic Book Publishing Corporation, 2009.

BECOME BETTER ACQUAINTED WITH YOUR BIBLE

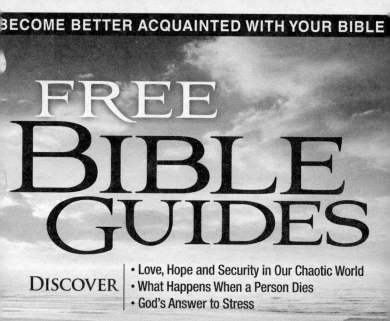

FREE
BIBLE
GUIDES

DISCOVER
- Love, Hope and Security in Our Chaotic World
- What Happens When a Person Dies
- God's Answer to Stress

Fill in the coupon below and mail it in. Or, sign up online at **www.bibleschools.com/request** or call **1-888-456-7933** and your first guide will arrive soon.

✓ YES!

I would like to receive the FREE Bible Guides

DISCOVER
BIBLE SCHOOL
O Box 999
oveland, CO 80539-0999

Name

Address

City   State/Province   Zip/Postal Code

Phone Number (optional)

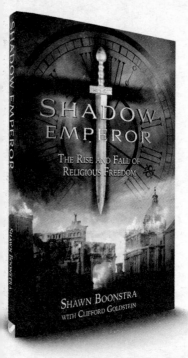

BORN UNDER THE CLOUD
OF ILLEGITIMACY.
HIS REAL FATHER
FAR MORE POWERFUL
THAN ANYONE COULD
IMAGINE.
THE UNLIKELY KING
WHO IGNITED A GLOBAL
MOVEMENT.
THE WORLD FOREVER
CHANGED.
HIS LEGACY - AN EMPIRE
REACHING ACROSS
CENTURIES.
HIS NAME?
CONSTANTINE.
IT'S NOT WHAT YOU'VE
BEEN TOLD.

In this book, Pastor Shawn Boonstra reveals the continuing rise and fall of religious freedom caused by this Shadow Emperor. And he lays out the choice each of us faces: will we continue to live in the shadow empire of Constantine, or walk in the light of Jesus?

Don't miss this intriguing study of history, prophecy and religious liberty!

Order Your Copy Now
Phone: (844) 822-2943
Online: store.vop.com